You Can Make This!

ALSO BY ANGELA KINSEY

The Office BFFS (with Jenna Fischer)

You Can Make This!

More Than 100 Family Favorite Recipes

Angela Kinsey & Joshua Snyder

GALLERY BOOKS

New York   Amsterdam/Antwerp   London   Toronto   Sydney/Melbourne   New Delhi

GALLERY BOOKS
An Imprint of Simon & Schuster, LLC
1230 Avenue of the Americas
New York, NY 10020

First Gallery Books hardcover edition October 2025

GALLERY BOOKS and colophon are registered trademarks of Simon & Schuster, LLC

For information about special discounts for bulk purchases, please contact Simon & Schuster Special Sales at 1-866-506-1949 or business@simonandschuster.com.

The Simon & Schuster Speakers Bureau can bring authors to your live event. For more information or to book an event, contact the Simon & Schuster Speakers Bureau at 1-866-248-3049 or visit our website at www.simonspeakers.com.

Interior design by Laura Palese
Interior photographs by Victoria Wall Harris

Manufactured in the United States of America

10 9 8 7 6 5 4 3 2 1

Library of Congress Control Number: 2025004917

ISBN 978-1-6680-6968-4
ISBN 978-1-6680-6969-1 (ebook)

This book is dedicated to our kids, Isabel, Jack, and Cade.
We will always hold dear the time we spend together in the kitchen.

Contents

Dinners

Cookies

Brownies and Bars

Cakes and Cupcakes

Pies and Puddings

Frozen Desserts and Sweet Snacks

AUTHORS' NOTE

A quick note for family we have in Colorado and others in mountain regions: Cooking and baking at high altitudes require a few adjustments, and it may take some trial and error to get them just right. For cooking, water boils at a lower temperature, so extend cooking times and add extra liquid to prevent drying out. For baking, reduce the amount of sugar slightly, add a little more flour for structure, and increase the oven temperature by 15 to 25°F. to help baked goods set before overexpanding. Additionally, reduce the amount of baking soda or baking powder by ⅛ to ¼ teaspoon per teaspoon to prevent overexpansion and collapsing. Happy cooking and baking!

Introduction

Hi there! We're Joshua Snyder and Angela Kinsey—Josh and Ange to friends and family, and since you'll be spending time with us in our kitchen, that includes you! Welcome to our cookbook. As a husband-and-wife team who loves to cook and bake, we're so excited to share our favorite family recipes with you, but first, here's a little about us.

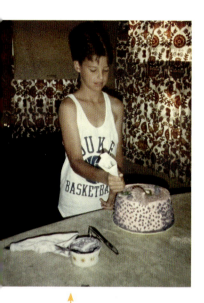

JOSH GREW UP IN both Kansas and Colorado and learned early on how to navigate life with family in two states. His family was full of DIYers, and because the kitchen was always at the heart of it all, there was a real can-do attitude at the center of his family's relationship with cooking and baking. Josh still has this instinct—so often, when one of us tastes something delicious at a new restaurant or bakery, Josh quickly sets to work reverse engineering a recipe for us to make at home. Josh's dad was known for his cake-making skills, and it's clear that some of his knack for baking and decorating rubbed off on Josh. From a young age, Josh was drawn to the kitchen, diving into cooking experiments ranging from quirky hors d'oeuvres he'd serve to his sisters as a predinner snack to more ambitious projects such as homemade caramel (which often left a sticky mess for his mom to clean up). Yet she always encouraged him and his sisters to try new recipes. The kitchen became Josh's happy place—a space in which to be creative, experiment with taste, and hone his skills. Whether he was helping Grandma Snyder make her famous mints for church or pitching in with dinner alongside his mom and sisters, Josh practiced his skills during these family moments.

JOSH *learning how to* DECORATE A CAKE *at his* Grandma Snyder's.

ANGELA
hamming
it up *for her*
SISTERS

MEANWHILE, ANGE GREW UP in Indonesia. Her parents, originally from Texas, were living in Louisiana when her dad's job took the family to Jakarta.

As a kid, she ate all kinds of food, from her mom's spicy Cajun Gumbo to her dad's Spam Surprise (yes, you read that correctly; her dad loved Spam and would fry it up for his girls) to dishes from Southeast Asia. On the weekends in Jakarta, Angela's mom would take her to the food markets, where there was always something new to try. Both of her parents regarded dinnertime as a special time; no matter what everyone had going on during the day, dinner was when the family came together. The youngest of four girls, Angela was too little to help at mealtimes, so her sisters would sit her on the countertop and let her play with pots and pans. There was a lot of laughter and silliness with four sisters in the kitchen. For Ange, cooking meant being together as a family, enjoying one another's company, and helping out however you could—even if you were the youngest and still learning. You could say that from an early age, the kitchen was her happy place, too.

It would be years before we met, but when we did, we instantly felt at home with each other. Meeting later in life, we had to figure out how to date while coordinating our busy lives as single parents.

That meant a lot of simple date nights over dinner at one of our houses. We cooked and baked a lot together in those early days. Our whole courtship happened in the kitchen, and we fell in love in those small moments. Cooking together is still our favorite part of the day. Every evening, we meet in the kitchen. We put work away, and we talk and cook while the kids bounce in and out as they finish their homework. Then we all sit down together for dinner. It's how we catch up at the end of a hectic day.

With three kids, two cats, and two dogs, our house is filled with what we call "delightful chaos." Amid all the hustle and bustle, we make it a point to gather around the table for meals.

For us, cooking isn't just about food; it's about spending time together, making memories, and getting the kids involved in the process. When we blended our families, we discovered that cooking and baking together were the perfect way to bring everyone closer. Our kitchen is more than just a room; it's the heart of our home. The kitchen is where everything happens, whether it's heart-to-heart talks over dinner, baking snickerdoodles with Cade, belting out Taylor Swift songs with Isabel, or listening to Jack strum his guitar.

We never imagined that we'd be sharing our love of cooking and baking for a living, but a few years ago, friends encouraged us to give it a shot. So in 2016, we decided to share our love of all things food with the world through our YouTube series, *Baking with Josh & Ange*.

The response to *Baking with Josh & Ange* has been more amazing than we ever expected. What started as a fun project in our kitchen has grown into something so much bigger: hundreds of recipes, a loyal audience, and now this cookbook. It's been so meaningful to see how something we created together has connected with so many people, bringing joy, laughter, and a love of baking into their kitchens. Those of you who follow us on YouTube or Instagram have probably seen some of our videos. After watching them, you'll know quickly which one of us is a natural in the kitchen and which one had some learning to do. But here's the beauty of cooking and baking: It is never too late to learn!

This cookbook is the culmination of everything we've built together. It's been a long journey, from filming in our kitchen with kids and pets running around to building a website full of recipes to where we are now. Through it all, our love of each other, of food, and of the process has stayed the same. No matter how busy life gets, we'll always find time to come back to the kitchen. It's where we started, and it's where we'll always feel at home.

Angela's
THE OFFICE
CASTMATES
stop by to
BAKE with us.

You Can Make This! is packed with easy-to-make recipes for all skill levels, along with our personal stories and family photos. We get it—cooking and baking can be intimidating, especially if you're new to it. That's why we've made sure that all the recipes in this book are as easy and approachable as possible. *You Can Make This!* is all about food, family, and fun! We want you to feel as though you're home with us, chatting in the kitchen while we whip up something delicious. And yes, there will be plenty of desserts because we *love* desserts! These recipes are our family's favorites—some passed down through generations and others we've created ourselves. For us, a family recipe is more than just a list of ingredients; it's a way to honor the past and create new traditions. Whether you're craving something old school such as Grandma Snyder's Brown Sugar Squares or something new such as Birthday Cake Crinkle Cookies, you'll find it here.

We hope you'll join us in the kitchen and make some delicious memories with your loved ones. Let's get started!

Ange & Josh

Breakfasts

Bakery-Style
GRANOLA

Not to brag, but my granola has become pretty famous with our family, friends, and Angela's tennis gals. A few years ago, Angela brought home a $12 bag of granola from a fancy French café, and our whole family loved it! I made it my mission to re-create the delicious granola at home on a budget, and my version may even surpass the original! It is also the perfect gift; we've given it to teachers and neighbors, taken it to brunches, and packaged it for holiday Christmas parties. —**J**

4 cups old-fashioned oats

1 cup raw pecans, coarsely chopped

½ cup sliced raw almonds

½ cup raw sunflower seeds

½ cup unsweetened flaked coconut

¼ cup raw pepitas

⅓ cup canola oil

⅓ cup honey

⅓ cup pure maple syrup

⅓ cup light brown sugar, packed

½ teaspoon sea salt

Flaky sea salt, for topping (optional)

1 Preheat your oven to 300°F. Line an 18-by-13-inch baking sheet with parchment paper. This will make cleaning up a breeze. Set aside.

2 In a large bowl, combine the oats, pecans, almonds, sunflower seeds, coconut, and pepitas.

3 In a medium microwave-safe bowl, combine the oil, honey, maple syrup, brown sugar, and sea salt. Heat in the microwave for about 45 seconds on high power. Remove from the microwave and stir until the brown sugar has dissolved. Pour the syrup mixture over the oat mixture and stir until everything is evenly coated.

4 Spread the granola onto the prepared baking sheet, taking care to create a nice, uniform layer so that the granola bakes evenly and doesn't end up soggy.

5 Bake for 30 minutes. Remove the granola from the oven and flip it in sections using a spatula. Being cautious of the hot pan, use a piece of parchment paper to press down firmly on the granola so it forms a solid, even layer.

6 Pop the baking sheet back into the oven and bake for another 30 to 35 minutes, rotating the pan halfway through, until golden brown.

7 Remove the granola from the oven. If you'd like, sprinkle some flaky sea salt over the top. Allow to cool completely, about 1 hour. Once cooled, break into 4- to 6-inch chunks and store in an airtight container to keep it fresh for up to two weeks.

Overnight DENVER EGG CASSEROLE

Here's a dish I make when hosting big Sunday brunches. Imagine a Denver omelet: fluffy eggs filled with gooey melted cheese, diced green peppers, onions, and savory chunks of ham. Now throw it all into a casserole dish. This is a true showstopper—simple to prepare but oh, so delicious. Make it the night before, bake it in the morning, and share it with friends at brunch. And maybe add some mimosas! (This dish is also easy to make without the ham for your vegetarian friends.) —**A**

6 cups cubed bread (French or whole wheat, cut into 1-inch cubes)

1 tablespoon extra-virgin olive oil

1 medium yellow onion, diced

1 green bell pepper, diced

1 red bell pepper, diced

1 teaspoon salt

1 teaspoon freshly ground black pepper

8 large eggs

2 cups milk (2% or whole)

1 teaspoon ground dry mustard

1 (4-ounce) can diced green chiles

1½ cups diced ham

2 cups shredded cheddar cheese

1 Preheat your oven to 250°F. Toast the cubed bread on a baking sheet for 10 minutes. Remove from the oven and set aside.

2 Grease a 13-by-9-inch baking dish with nonstick spray, cooking spray, or butter. Set aside.

3 In a medium skillet, heat the olive oil over medium heat until shimmering. Add the onion and bell peppers and sauté until soft and tender, 6 to 7 minutes. Season with the salt and pepper. Remove from heat.

4 In a large bowl, whisk together the eggs, milk, and dry mustard until the mixture is smooth and well combined. Then stir in the green chiles.

5 Spread the cubed toasted bread in the bottom of the prepared baking dish. Add half of the diced ham, half of the sautéed veggies, and half of the cheese. Gently pour the egg mixture over the casserole layers. Top with the remaining ham, veggies, and a final layer of cheese.

6 Cover the dish with plastic wrap and refrigerate. If you're in a pinch for time, a minimum of 3 hours will suffice, but overnight is best.

7 When you're ready to bake, remove the baking dish from the refrigerator and let it sit at room temperature for 30 minutes. Preheat your oven to 350°F.

8 Remove the plastic wrap and bake the casserole for 40 to 45 minutes, until it's set and golden on top. Allow the casserole to rest for 5 minutes before serving.

Overnight COFFEE CAKE

Overnight Coffee Cake holds a special place in my heart. When I was growing up, my mom used to make it for me and my sisters every year on Christmas morning. To this day, the aroma of this coffee cake brings back warm memories from my childhood, and now it's a tradition I continue with my own family. It's so easy; just prep it the night before, and pop it into the oven in the morning. No stress, just pure holiday joy for a cozy Christmas morning. I can't help but feel grateful for this cherished tradition passed down from my mom to my own family. Maybe someday our kids will make this same recipe for their families! —J

For the cake

2¾ cups all-purpose flour

1½ teaspoons baking powder

1 teaspoon baking soda

2 teaspoons ground cinnamon

1 teaspoon ground nutmeg

¾ teaspoon salt

1 cup unsalted butter, softened

1½ cups granulated sugar

¾ cup light brown sugar, packed

3 large eggs, room temperature

1½ teaspoons vanilla extract

¾ cup milk (2% or whole), room temperature

¾ cup Greek yogurt, room temperature

For the cinnamon crumb

½ cup unsalted butter, softened

1½ cups all-purpose flour

1 cup light brown sugar, packed

2 teaspoons ground cinnamon

½ teaspoon salt

For the glaze

1 cup powdered sugar

1 to 2 tablespoons milk (2% or whole)

1 **Make the cake:** Grease a 13-by-9-inch baking dish with nonstick spray or cooking spray and set aside.

2 In a medium bowl, whisk together the flour, baking powder, baking soda, cinnamon, nutmeg, and salt. Set aside.

3 In the bowl of a stand mixer fitted with a paddle attachment or a large bowl using a hand mixer, beat the butter until creamy. Add the granulated sugar and brown sugar and beat for 2 to 3 minutes, until light and fluffy. Add the eggs one at a time, beating after each addition, then add the vanilla extract and beat until smooth. Turn the mixer to low. Add half of the flour mixture, beating until almost combined. Add the milk, then the remaining flour mixture, continuing to beat on low. Finally, add the Greek yogurt and beat until the batter is smooth and uniform. Add the batter to the prepared baking dish.

4 Tightly cover the baking dish with plastic wrap and refrigerate it overnight to allow the flavors to meld and the batter to rise.

5 **Make the cinnamon crumb:** To a medium bowl, add the butter, flour, brown sugar, cinnamon, and salt. Mix with a pastry cutter until uniform and crumbly. Cover tightly with plastic wrap and store in the refrigerator overnight.

6 **Finish the cake:** The next morning, remove the baking dish from the refrigerator and let it sit at room temperature for 30 minutes.

7 Preheat your oven to 350°F.

8 Remove the plastic wrap and bake for 25 minutes. Carefully remove from the oven and sprinkle the crumb topping evenly over the top. Return to the oven and bake for another 20 to 25 minutes, until a toothpick inserted in the center comes out clean. Allow to cool for 10 minutes.

9 **Make the glaze:** In a medium bowl, whisk together the powdered sugar and milk until smooth. Drizzle the glaze over the coffee cake. If you want the glaze to soak into the cake, add the glaze while the cake is still warm. If you prefer a more pronounced glaze layer, wait until the cake is completely cool. Allow the glaze to set for 10 minutes before slicing and serving the cake.

Make this!

You can substitute an equal amount of sour cream for the Greek yogurt.

" *the* AROMA *of this* coffee cake *brings back* WARM MEMORIES

Hash Brown
BREAKFAST
MUFFINS

Are you tired of the same old boring breakfast choices? Cereal, eggs, yogurt . . . they can start to blend together after a while. That's where these delicious hash brown breakfast muffins come in. They are the perfect savory single-serving breakfast item, similar to the expensive egg cups at your local coffee shop. These muffins make a great snack or addition to a brunch spread. Reheat them in the microwave for a quick and easy meal, or pop them into the oven for a crisp texture.

For the hash brown cups

20 ounces frozen shredded hash browns, thawed

½ cup shredded cheddar cheese

1 large egg

1 tablespoon extra-virgin olive oil

½ teaspoon salt

¼ teaspoon freshly ground black pepper

For the egg filling

4 large eggs

½ cup shredded cheddar cheese

¼ cup milk (2% or whole)

1 (4-ounce) can diced green chiles

¼ cup diced red onion

1 teaspoon salt

½ teaspoon freshly ground black pepper

Sour cream and sliced green onion, for topping

1 **Make the hash brown cups:** Preheat your oven to 400°F. Generously grease a 12-cup muffin tin with nonstick spray or cooking spray.

2 In a large bowl, mix the hash browns, cheese, egg, olive oil, salt, and pepper. Evenly divide the mixture into the muffin cups, pressing it firmly into the bottom of each cup and halfway up the sides.

3 Bake for about 15 minutes, until the edges are crispy. Remove from the oven and set aside.

4 **Make the egg filling:** Whisk the eggs in a large bowl. Stir in the cheese, milk, green chiles, and red onion. Season with the salt and pepper.

5 **Finish the hash brown cups:** Fill the hash brown cups evenly with the egg mixture.

6 Bake for about 15 minutes, until the egg filling is fully set. Allow the muffins to cool in the tin for about 5 minutes. Serve warm and top with sour cream and green onion.

Buttermilk WAFFLES

Who doesn't love waking up to the aroma of freshly made buttermilk waffles? They're a must-have on lazy Sunday mornings and easy to reheat on hectic school days. We like to top them with a little powdered sugar and maple syrup (Cade's favorite) or honey butter (Isabel's favorite). And Jack? Well, he likes just a little extra powdered sugar on top.

2 cups all-purpose flour

2 tablespoons granulated sugar

2 teaspoons baking powder

1 teaspoon baking soda

1 teaspoon salt

2 large eggs, room temperature

2 cups buttermilk, room temperature

6 tablespoons unsalted butter, melted and cooled to room temperature

2 teaspoons vanilla extract

Nonstick or cooking spray, for greasing waffle maker

Powdered sugar, maple syrup, fresh berries, or whipped cream, for serving

1 In a large bowl, combine the flour, sugar, baking powder, baking soda, and salt. Give it a few good whisks and set it aside.

2 In a medium bowl, whisk together the eggs, buttermilk, butter, and vanilla extract until frothy and well-blended.

3 Add the buttermilk mixture to the flour mixture, whisking until just combined. A few lumps in the batter are totally fine. Let the batter sit while you preheat your waffle maker.

4 Preheat your waffle maker according to the manufacturer's instructions and lightly grease it with nonstick spray or cooking spray. Using ⅓ to ½ cup of batter per waffle, cook each waffle for 2 to 3 minutes, until golden brown and crisp. Serve immediately with powdered sugar, maple syrup, fresh berries, or whipped cream.

Make this!

To make 1 cup of buttermilk, combine 1 cup whole milk with 2 teaspoons lemon juice or vinegar and stir until combined.

Lemon Blueberry CRUMB CAKE

Our family loves lemons, which is convenient since we have several lemon trees in our backyard. And when we run out of lemons, our neighbor Karen lets us pick hers. (Thanks, Karen!) This cake combines all of our favorite breakfast bakes: blueberry muffins, lemon loaves, and coffee cake. It's the perfect treat for a spring or summer morning. A word of wisdom: If you're using frozen blueberries, do not thaw them before adding to the batter. This will prevent their color from bleeding.

For the topping

½ cup all-purpose flour

½ cup granulated sugar

½ teaspoon salt

1 tablespoon lemon zest

¼ cup cold unsalted butter, cut into ¼-inch cubes

For the cake

1 cup fresh or frozen blueberries

2 cups plus 2 tablespoons all-purpose flour, divided

2 teaspoons baking powder

½ teaspoon baking soda

½ teaspoon salt

½ cup unsalted butter, room temperature

1 cup granulated sugar

2 large eggs, room temperature

1 teaspoon vanilla extract

½ cup Greek yogurt

¼ cup fresh lemon juice

1 tablespoon lemon zest

For the glaze

1 cup powdered sugar

2 teaspoons lemon juice

Make this!

You can substitute an equal amount of sour cream for the Greek yogurt.

1 **Make the topping:** Combine the flour, sugar, salt, lemon zest, and butter in a small bowl. With a pastry cutter or fork, combine until the mixture comes together into pea-size crumbs and set aside.

2 **Make the cake:** Preheat your oven to 350°F. Lightly grease a 9-inch-square baking pan and line it with parchment paper.

3 In a small bowl, toss the blueberries with 2 tablespoons of flour until they are evenly coated. Set aside.

4 In a medium bowl, whisk together 2 cups of flour with the baking powder, baking soda, and salt.

5 In the bowl of a stand mixer fitted with a paddle attachment or in a large bowl using a hand mixer, cream together the butter and sugar until the mixture is light and fluffy, 2 to 3 minutes. Reduce speed to medium. Add the eggs, one at a time, mixing after each edition, then the vanilla extract, and mix until combined. Turn the mixer to low and add the Greek yogurt, lemon juice, and lemon zest and beat until incorporated. Stop the mixer and scrape down the sides and bottom of the bowl with a rubber spatula. Turn the mixer to low and slowly add the flour mixture, mixing until just combined. Using a spatula, gently fold the flour-coated blueberries into the batter.

Recipe Continues

6 Transfer the batter into the prepared baking pan and sprinkle the crumb topping over the top.

7 Bake for 40 to 45 minutes, until a toothpick inserted into the center of the cake comes out clean. Allow the cake to cool in the pan for 10 to 15 minutes. Transfer it to a wire rack to cool completely.

8 Make the glaze: In a medium bowl, whisk together the powdered sugar and lemon juice. Drizzle the glaze over the coffee cake. If you want the glaze to soak into the cake add the glaze while the cake is still warm. If you prefer a more pronounced glaze layer, wait until the cake is completely cool. Allow the glaze to set for 10 minutes before slicing and serving.

JOSH *and* ISABEL *in the* kitchen

Ultimate Overnight
FRENCH TOAST CASSEROLE

My mom used to make us French toast using big Texas bread. And let me tell you, it was *the best.* Just an egg, milk, cinnamon, and bread . . . a few minutes on the skillet . . . topped with a little butter and sprinkled with sugar. Yum! But check this out: Josh found a way to take regular French toast and make it even better. It's a fancy version with a cinnamon crumble topping, all baked together in a casserole dish. It's the perfect option for lazy weekends when family is in town and you need to feed a crowd. —**A**

For the French toast

½ **large loaf French bread (about 8 ounces), cut into 1-inch cubes**

4 **large eggs, room temperature**

1 **cup milk (2% or whole), room temperature**

¼ **cup light brown sugar, packed**

2 **teaspoons vanilla extract**

½ **teaspoon ground cinnamon**

½ **teaspoon salt**

For the topping

¼ **cup unsalted butter, cold and diced into small pieces**

¼ **cup all-purpose flour**

¼ **cup brown sugar, packed**

½ **teaspoon ground cinnamon**

½ **teaspoon salt**

Powdered sugar and maple syrup, for serving

1 **Make the French toast:** Preheat your oven to 250°F. Grease an 8-inch-square baking dish with nonstick spray, cooking spray, or butter. Set aside.

2 Toast the cubed bread on a baking sheet for 10 minutes. Remove from the oven and set aside to cool for 5 minutes.

3 Place the bread cubes into the prepared baking dish.

4 In a medium bowl, whisk together the eggs, milk, brown sugar, vanilla extract, cinnamon, and salt. Pour evenly over the bread and, with your fingers, gently press down on the bread cubes so that every piece is submerged and soaking up the liquid. Cover the dish with plastic wrap and refrigerate. Overnight is ideal for best results, but if time is tight, 3 hours is fine.

5 **Make the topping:** Combine the butter, flour, brown sugar, cinnamon, and salt in a small bowl and, using a pastry cutter or fork, combine until you have crumbs the size of small peas. Cover and transfer to the refrigerator until the casserole is ready to bake.

6 **Finish the French toast:** Preheat your oven to 350°F. Remove the casserole and the crumb topping from the refrigerator and allow to sit at room temperature for 30 minutes. Remove the plastic wrap and sprinkle the crumb topping over the bread.

7 Bake uncovered for 45 to 55 minutes, until the top is golden and set with a slight wobble. Let cool slightly, then dust with powdered sugar. Serve with maple syrup.

Sausage and Egg CRESCENT ROLL BREAKFAST PIZZA

I'm aware that this might not be a popular opinion, but I just don't enjoy pizza. It's never been my thing. However, breakfast pizza is my one exception. I can never resist breakfast food, no matter what time of day it is. This delicious, easy-to-make breakfast pizza has become my go-to dish for weekend brunches and sometimes even weeknight dinners. —**J**

For the cheese sauce

1 tablespoon unsalted butter

1 tablespoon all-purpose flour

1 cup milk (2% or whole)

½ cup shredded cheddar cheese

¾ teaspoon salt

½ teaspoon freshly ground black pepper

For the cooked toppings

1 tablespoon plus 1 teaspoon extra-virgin olive oil, divided

12 ounces breakfast sausage, casings removed

1 cup frozen hash browns, thawed

6 large eggs

¼ cup milk (2% or whole)

¾ teaspoon salt

½ teaspoon freshly ground black pepper

For the pizza base

1 (8-ounce) can refrigerated crescent rolls

½ red bell pepper, diced

½ green bell pepper, diced

½ medium yellow onion, diced

1 cup shredded mozzarella

½ cup shredded cheddar cheese

2 green onions, sliced

1 Preheat your oven to 375°F. Line a 15-by-10-inch baking sheet with parchment paper and spray with nonstick spray or cooking spray. Set aside.

2 **Make the cheese sauce:** In a small saucepan, melt the butter over medium heat. Stir in the flour and cook for 1 minute. Gradually whisk in the milk. Bring to a boil, whisking constantly, and cook until thickened, 3 to 4 minutes. Remove from heat, stir in the cheddar cheese, and season with the salt and pepper. Stir until the cheese has melted and the mixture is smooth. Set aside to cool slightly.

3 **Cook the toppings:** In a medium skillet, heat 1 tablespoon of olive oil over medium heat until shimmering. Add the breakfast sausage and cook while breaking apart the sausage with a wooden spoon for 6 to 8 minutes, until the sausage is crumbled and well browned. Transfer the sausage to a plate and set aside. Add the thawed hash browns to the skillet and sauté for 5 to 6 minutes, until they begin to crisp up and get some color. Remove to a second plate.

4 In a large bowl, whisk the eggs with the milk and season with the salt and pepper. To the skillet you used to cook the sausage and hash browns, add the 1 teaspoon of oil and turn the heat to medium low.

Add the egg mixture to the skillet and scramble for 1 to 2 minutes, until the eggs are just set but still moist. Remove from heat slightly undercooked since they'll cook more in the oven.

5 **Make the pizza:** Unroll the crescent roll dough in one large sheet and place on the prepared baking sheet. Press and work the crescent dough into the bottom of the pan, gently stretching it as needed to cover the surface and slightly up the sides. Pinch the seams together to form a smooth, even layer.

6 Spread the cheese sauce evenly over the crescent roll dough.

7 Layer the scrambled eggs, sausage, and hash browns on top of the prepared dough. Sprinkle the bell peppers and yellow onion over the hash browns. Top evenly with the mozzarella and cheddar cheese.

8 Bake in the preheated oven for 25 to 30 minutes, or until the cheese is bubbly and the edges of the crescent roll crust are golden brown. Remove the pizza from the oven and let cool for a few minutes to allow the cheese sauce to set. Sprinkle the green onions over the top. Transfer to a cutting board, slice, and serve warm.

MONKEY BREAD

Monkey Bread was one of my mom's go-to recipes for breakfast. I can still remember how it smelled when I walked into the kitchen those mornings. With its interwoven dough and caramel sauce, it looked and tasted delicious. Our kids love it, too, so much so that Cade learned the recipe and now makes it for us for breakfast! Feel free to add your own twist to the recipe by incorporating nuts, raisins, or even small chunks of apple into the sugar and cinnamon mixture for added texture and flavor. —J

2 (16.3-ounce) cans refrigerated biscuit dough

1 cup granulated sugar

2 teaspoons ground cinnamon

¾ cup unsalted butter

¾ cup light brown sugar, packed

1 Preheat your oven to 350°F. Grease a 10-inch Bundt pan with nonstick or cooking spray.

2 Slice each biscuit into quarters. You should have 64 pieces.

3 To a gallon-size zip-top bag or large bowl, add the sugar and cinnamon. Shake to combine. Add the biscuit quarters to the cinnamon-sugar mixture in batches and shake or toss until coated. Loosely arrange the biscuit pieces in the Bundt pan.

4 In a small saucepan, melt the butter over medium heat. Stir in the brown sugar. When the mixture is smooth and bubbling, remove from heat. Slowly pour over the biscuits.

5 Bake for 30 to 35 minutes, until the top is golden brown. Allow the bread to cool in the pan for about 5 minutes. Invert the still-warm bread onto a large plate or platter by placing the plate over the Bundt pan and flipping to release. Serve warm.

" Monkey Bread *is always* A BIG HIT!

Muffins

CHOCOLATE CHIP *Muffins*

This book has a bunch of recipes that the kids and I tested together. This is one that Cade really wanted to include. He went to a bakery a few years ago and came home with a chocolate chip muffin that he liked but was determined to make a better version of. After lots of experimenting, we finally got the perfect combo of flavors. Then we topped it off with some crunchy sugar, and *boom!*—our muffins were even better than the bakery's! Now they're a staple in our house thanks to Cade. Way to go, buddy! —**J**

2¾ cups all-purpose flour

2 teaspoons baking powder

1 teaspoon baking soda

1 teaspoon ground cinnamon

¼ teaspoon ground nutmeg

½ teaspoon salt

½ cup canola oil

¼ cup unsalted butter, melted and cooled to room temperature

1 cup granulated sugar

2 large eggs, room temperature

½ cup Greek yogurt, room temperature

1 cup milk (2% or whole), room temperature

1 teaspoon vanilla extract

1 cup semisweet chocolate chips

Coarse sugar, for sprinkling

1 Preheat your oven to 400°F. Line a 12-cup muffin tin with baking cups or grease with nonstick spray or cooking spray and set aside.

2 In a large bowl, whisk together the flour, baking powder, baking soda, cinnamon, nutmeg, and salt. Make a well in the center.

3 In a large bowl, whisk together the oil, butter, and sugar until completely combined. Whisk in the eggs, Greek yogurt, milk, and vanilla extract until the mixture is uniform. Pour the wet ingredients into the well in the dry ingredients and mix, using a wooden spoon or spatula, until just combined. Gently fold in the chocolate chips, making sure they are evenly distributed throughout the batter, being careful not to overmix.

4 Fill each muffin cup about three quarters full. A ¼-cup measuring cup works well for this. Sprinkle each cup generously with coarse sugar.

5 Bake at 400°F for 5 minutes, then reduce the temperature to 350°F and bake for an additional 15 to 18 minutes or until a toothpick inserted into the center comes out clean. Let the muffins cool in the tin for 5 minutes before transferring to a wire rack.

Make this!

You can easily make 9 jumbo muffins with this recipe using a jumbo muffin tin. Bake for 10 minutes at 400°F, then lower the oven temperature to 350°F and continue baking for 20 to 25 minutes.

BANANA BREAD CRUMB *Muffins*

These yummy treats make use of those mushy brown bananas that always seem to live in our kitchen. Our kids love these muffins so much, Isabel even requested them for her birthday breakfast. We come back to these muffins time and time again—they're just that good! —**A**

For the topping

3 tablespoons unsalted butter, softened

½ cup light brown sugar, packed

¼ cup all-purpose flour

¼ cup granulated sugar

1½ teaspoons ground cinnamon

½ teaspoon salt

For the muffins

1½ cups all-purpose flour

1 teaspoon ground cinnamon

½ teaspoon baking powder

½ teaspoon baking soda

½ teaspoon salt

⅓ cup canola oil

3 to 4 medium ripe bananas, mashed (about 1½ cups)

½ cup granulated sugar

¼ cup light brown sugar, packed

1 large egg, beaten

1½ teaspoons vanilla extract

1 **Make the topping:** To a small bowl, add the butter, brown sugar, flour, granulated sugar, cinnamon, and salt. Mix with a pastry cutter or fork until it is a coarse, sandy texture. Set aside.

2 **Make the muffins:** Preheat your oven to 375°F. Line a 12-cup muffin tin with paper liners.

3 In a medium bowl, whisk together the flour, cinnamon, baking powder, baking soda, and salt.

4 To a large bowl, add the oil, bananas, granulated sugar, and brown sugar. Mix using a wooden spoon or spatula until the mixture has a uniform consistency. Don't worry if the mixture looks a bit lumpy; that's totally normal. Add the egg and vanilla extract to the banana mixture and mix well until incorporated. Slowly add the dry ingredients and stir until just combined.

5 Fill each muffin cup about three quarters full. A ¼-cup measuring cup works well for this. Sprinkle the crumb topping evenly over the muffin batter.

6 Bake for 18 to 20 minutes, until a toothpick inserted in the middle comes out clean. Cool completely on a wire rack.

ORANGE POPPY SEED *Muffins*

When we moved into our house, we planted a tiny orange tree in the front yard. For years it barely grew and didn't produce any fruit, and then one year, it took off! We had so many oranges that I lined them up on the dining table and sent a picture to my mom in Texas. We made orange juice, orange popsicles, you name it, and we still had so many oranges. I told Josh he had to come up with a recipe. These delicious muffins blend the tangy sweetness of oranges with the satisfying crunch of poppy seeds. (And we still have more oranges!) —**A**

For the muffins

2¼ cups all-purpose flour

2 teaspoons baking powder

¼ teaspoon baking soda

1 teaspoon salt

¾ cup granulated sugar

1 tablespoon orange zest

¾ cup Greek yogurt

½ cup fresh orange juice (from about 2 medium oranges)

½ cup canola oil

2 large eggs, room temperature

1½ teaspoons pure vanilla extract

½ teaspoon almond extract

2 tablespoons poppy seeds

For the simple syrup

½ cup water

½ cup granulated sugar

3 tablespoons freshly squeezed orange juice

2 (2-by-4-inch) strips of orange peel (from about ½ orange), pith removed

For the glaze

2 cups powdered sugar

1 tablespoon orange zest

2 to 3 tablespoons freshly squeezed orange juice

¼ teaspoon almond extract

1 **Make the muffins:** Preheat your oven to 350°F. Line a 12-cup muffin tin with baking cups or grease with nonstick spray or cooking spray and set aside.

2 In a large bowl, whisk together the flour, baking powder, baking soda, and salt. Make a well in the center.

3 In a second large bowl, combine the sugar and orange zest. Rub together with your fingers until the mixture becomes fragrant. Add the Greek yogurt, orange juice, oil, eggs, vanilla extract, and almond extract. Whisk until well combined.

4 Pour the wet ingredients into the well in the dry ingredients and mix until just combined. Fold in the poppy seeds, making sure they are evenly distributed throughout the batter and being careful not to overmix.

5 Fill each muffin cup about three quarters full. A ¼-cup measuring cup works well for this. Bake for 20 to 25 minutes, until the muffins are golden brown on the edges and a toothpick inserted into one comes out clean. Set aside to cool.

Recipe Continues

> *When we* moved into our HOUSE, *we* planted a tiny ORANGE TREE *in the* front yard.

6 **Make the simple syrup:** In a small saucepan, combine the water, sugar, orange juice, and orange peel strips. Bring to a boil over medium heat, stirring occasionally, until the sugar dissolves. Reduce heat to medium low and let simmer for 5 minutes. Remove from heat and set aside to cool. Discard the orange peel.

7 **Make the glaze:** In a medium bowl, whisk together the powdered sugar, orange zest, orange juice, and almond extract until smooth.

8 **Finish the muffins:** Once the muffins are cool, brush them with the simple syrup. Drizzle the glaze over the top of the muffins and let them sit for about 30 minutes to allow the glaze to harden before serving.

Make this!

You'll have extra simple syrup left after making this recipe. If desired, you can save it and use it for cocktails, drizzle it over pancakes, or even keep it on hand for your next batch of muffins.

You can substitute an equal amount of sour cream for the Greek yogurt.

BLUEBERRY MUFFINS *with* STREUSEL TOPPING

I am pretty sure that this chapter is in the cookbook because I constantly want a muffin. And Josh knows the way to my heart, so he is always coming up with more muffin recipes! The man managed to take blueberry muffins to the next level: He added a mouthwatering crumble on top! These muffins are like little bites of Heaven. Thanks, babe. —A

For the streusel topping

½ cup all-purpose flour

½ cup granulated sugar

½ teaspoon salt

¼ cup unsalted butter

For the muffins

1½ cups (8 ounces) fresh or frozen blueberries

2½ cups all-purpose flour, divided

1 teaspoon cornstarch

2 teaspoons baking powder

1 teaspoon salt

¼ cup unsalted butter, melted and cooled to room temperature

¼ cup canola oil

1 cup granulated sugar

2 large eggs, room temperature

1 teaspoon vanilla extract

2 teaspoons lemon zest

¼ cup lemon juice

1 cup milk (2% or whole), room temperature

1 Make the streusel topping: In a medium bowl, combine the flour, sugar, salt, and butter with a fork until the mixture is crumbly. Set aside.

2 Make the muffins: Preheat your oven to 400°F. Line a 12-cup muffin tin with baking cups or grease with nonstick spray or cooking spray and set aside.

3 In a small bowl, toss together the blueberries and ¼ cup of flour until evenly coated.

4 In a medium bowl, whisk together the remaining 2¼ cups of flour, cornstarch, baking powder, and salt.

5 In a large bowl, whisk together the butter, oil, sugar, eggs, vanilla extract, lemon zest, and lemon juice until completely combined.

6 Add half of the flour mixture to the wet mixture and mix using a wooden spoon or spatula until combined. Stir in the milk, then the remaining flour mixture, and mix until almost combined. Gently fold in the flour-coated blueberries.

7 Spoon the batter into the prepared muffin cups, filling them three quarters full. A ¼-cup measuring cup works well for this. Generously sprinkle an even layer of the streusel topping on top of the batter.

8 Bake for 5 minutes at 400°F, then lower the oven temperature to 350°F and continue baking for 15 to 20 minutes, until a toothpick inserted into the center comes out clean. Remove from the oven and let cool in the tin for 5 minutes before releasing from the tin.

CARROT CAKE *Muffins* *with* CREAM CHEESE FILLING

Ange loves hosting a big Easter brunch for friends and family. She decorates the house and yard. (I cannot tell you how many little bunnies we have, but it's a lot.) It's festive and fun, and the kids love it. Last year I added these carrot cake muffins to our brunch menu, and they were a huge hit! Plus, they're a sneaky source of veggies on a holiday that is heavy on candy and chocolates. These muffins have just the right amount of moisture and spice to make them irresistible. And with their hidden sweet cream cheese filling, even the Easter Bunny approves. —J

For the filling

8 ounces cream cheese, softened

½ cup granulated sugar

½ teaspoon ground cinnamon

½ teaspoon vanilla extract

For the muffins

1¾ cups all-purpose flour

2 teaspoons ground cinnamon

1 teaspoon baking powder

½ teaspoon baking soda

½ teaspoon salt

½ teaspoon ground ginger

¼ teaspoon ground nutmeg

⅛ teaspoon ground cloves

½ cup canola oil

2 large eggs, room temperature

¼ cup buttermilk, room temperature

½ cup granulated sugar

¼ cup light brown sugar

2 teaspoons vanilla extract

1½ cups grated carrots

Coarse sugar, for topping

1 Make the filling: In a large bowl, using a handheld mixer or a stand mixer fitted with the whisk attachment, beat the cream cheese until creamy. Add the sugar, cinnamon, and vanilla extract, beating thoroughly until combined. Set aside.

2 Make the muffins: Preheat your oven to 400°F. Line a 12-cup muffin tin with baking cups or grease with nonstick spray or cooking spray.

3 In a medium bowl, whisk together the flour, cinnamon, baking powder, baking soda, salt, ginger, nutmeg, and cloves until well blended. Make a well in the center.

4 In a large bowl, whisk together the oil, eggs, buttermilk, granulated sugar, brown sugar, and vanilla extract. Pour the wet ingredients into the well in the dry ingredients and with a wooden spoon or spatula stir until just combined. Gently fold in the carrots, making sure they are evenly distributed throughout the batter and being careful not to overmix.

5 Fill each muffin cup about a third of the way. Spoon or pipe even dollops of the cream cheese mixture into the center of each muffin cup, then cover with the remaining batter. Sprinkle each muffin generously with coarse sugar.

6 Bake for 16 to 18 minutes, until the edges turn golden brown. Allow the muffins to cool on a wire rack for about 10 minutes before serving.

Make this!

To make 1 cup of buttermilk, combine 1 cup whole milk with 2 teaspoons lemon juice or vinegar and stir until combined.

66 It's FESTIVE *and* FUN, *and the* KIDS LOVE it.

Jalapeño and Honey CORNBREAD MUFFINS

My family is spread out between Texas and Louisiana, and every one of us has a signature cornbread recipe. Don't get me started on my mom's skillet cornbread, which she cooks in her leftover bacon grease. It is soooo good. I told Josh that as a Southern gal, I, too, needed a signature cornbread recipe. He took my favorite cornbread, added honey, and then made it into a muffin. (Does this man get me, or what?). Then, just as I thought it couldn't get better, he added jalapeños! The balance of savory and sweet flavors is perfection. Yeehaw! Enjoy! —**A**

1 tablespoon unsalted butter, plus 5 tablespoons melted and cooled to room temperature

2 fresh jalapeño peppers, seeded and diced

½ red bell pepper, seeded and diced

1¼ cups yellow cornmeal

¾ cup all-purpose flour

½ cup light brown sugar, packed

1 tablespoon baking powder

½ teaspoon salt

1 large egg, room temperature

1 large egg yolk, room temperature

½ cup buttermilk, room temperature

½ cup sour cream, room temperature

¼ cup honey

1 Preheat your oven to 400°F. Spray a 12-cup muffin tin with nonstick or cooking spray, or line with baking cups. Set aside.

2 In a small sauté pan, melt the 1 tablespoon of butter over medium heat. Once melted, add the jalapeños and bell pepper and sauté until soft, 4 to 5 minutes. Remove from heat.

3 In a large bowl, whisk together the cornmeal, flour, brown sugar, baking powder, and salt. Make a well in the center.

4 In a separate large bowl, whisk together the 5 tablespoons of melted butter, the egg, egg yolk, buttermilk, sour cream, and honey until combined.

5 Pour the wet ingredients into the well in the dry ingredients and using a wooden spoon or spatula mix until just combined. Gently fold in the sautéed peppers, making sure they are evenly distributed throughout the batter and being careful not to overmix.

6 Fill each muffin cup about three quarters full. A ¼-cup measuring cup works well for this. Bake for 13 to 15 minutes, or until a toothpick inserted in the center comes out clean. Let the muffins cool completely before removing them from the tin.

Make this!

To make 1 cup of buttermilk, combine 1 cup whole milk with 2 teaspoons lemon juice or vinegar and stir until combined.

MINI DOUGHNUT
Muffins

If you know my wife, you know how much she loves doughnuts. Well, when I told her that I was going to make a doughnut muffin, the celebration dance she did in the kitchen was epic. You would have thought she had won the Super Bowl. These little bites are the perfect indulgence. Hot out of the oven and dipped in butter and cinnamon sugar, it's hard to eat just one. —J

For the muffins
2½ cups all-purpose flour

1½ teaspoons baking powder

¼ teaspoon baking soda

1 teaspoon ground cinnamon

1 teaspoon ground nutmeg

¾ teaspoon salt

¼ cup unsalted butter, melted and cooled to room temperature

¼ cup canola oil

½ cup granulated sugar

½ cup brown sugar, packed

2 large eggs, room temperature

1 teaspoon vanilla extract

1 cup buttermilk, room temperature

For the coating
¼ cup unsalted butter, melted

¼ cup granulated sugar

2 teaspoons ground cinnamon

1 Make the muffins: Preheat your oven to 400°F. Grease two mini muffin tins with nonstick spray, cooking spray, or butter. Set aside.

2 In a medium bowl, whisk together the flour, baking powder, baking soda, cinnamon, nutmeg, and salt.

3 In the bowl of a stand mixer fitted with a paddle attachment or a large bowl with a hand mixer, beat the butter, oil, granulated sugar, and brown sugar until well combined, scraping down the sides of the bowl as needed. Turn speed to low and add the eggs one at a time, beating after each addition, then the vanilla extract. Add half of the flour mixture and beat until combined. Pour in the buttermilk, then the remaining flour mixture, and mix until just combined.

4 Using a spoon or an icing bag, fill the cups of the prepared mini muffin pans with batter about halfway. Bake each batch for 9 to 10 minutes, or until the edges turn a light golden brown. Remove from the oven and let cool in the pan for about 5 minutes. Remove from the tin.

5 Make the coating: To a medium bowl, add the melted butter. In a separate medium bowl, combine the sugar and cinnamon. Dunk each muffin into the butter and roll it through the cinnamon-sugar mixture until coated.

Make this!
To make 1 cup of buttermilk, combine 1 cup whole milk with 2 teaspoons lemon juice or vinegar and stir until combined.

Pumpkin Oatmeal CHOCOLATE CHIP MUFFINS

The average daily temperature in Los Angeles in October is 87°F. I used to set out pumpkins along our porch, but they would turn into mush from the heat, so I had to find other ways to get us into that "pumpkin season" spirit. I don't care how hot it is outside; our house is going to feel like fall, dang it! I put ceramic and plastic pumpkins everywhere. It might look a tad tacky, but it is definitely festive. And then Josh really brings on the fall flavors with these muffins (although they are a winner any time of year). Happy fall, y'all! —A

¾ cup all-purpose flour

2 teaspoons pumpkin pie spice

1 teaspoon baking powder

½ teaspoon baking soda

½ teaspoon salt

½ cup buttermilk, room temperature

½ cup pumpkin puree

¼ cup canola oil

½ cup light brown sugar, packed

½ cup pure maple syrup

1 large egg, room temperature

1 teaspoon vanilla extract

2 cups old-fashioned rolled oats

¾ cup semisweet chocolate chips

1 Preheat your oven to 350°F. Line a 12-cup muffin tin with baking cups or grease with nonstick spray or cooking spray. Set aside.

2 In a large bowl, whisk together the flour, pumpkin pie spice, baking powder, baking soda, and salt. Make a well in the center.

3 In another large bowl, whisk together the buttermilk, pumpkin puree, oil, brown sugar, maple syrup, egg, and vanilla extract.

4 Pour the wet ingredients into the well in the dry ingredients and mix with a wooden spoon or spatula until just combined. Fold in the oats and chocolate chips, making sure they are evenly distributed throughout the batter and being careful not to overmix.

5 Fill each muffin cup about three quarters full. A ¼-cup measuring cup works well for this. Bake for 20 to 25 minutes, until a toothpick inserted into the center comes out clean. Allow the muffins to cool in the pan for about 10 minutes.

Make this!

To make 1 cup of buttermilk, combine 1 cup whole milk with 2 teaspoons lemon juice or vinegar and stir until combined.

Dips, Appetizers, and Salads

SOUTHWEST SALAD *with* CHICKEN

When I was a kid, I was not a fan of salad. When I did have to eat one, I used salsa as the salad dressing. Now I enjoy eating salads, but I am still picky about the dressing. That's why I like the honey-lime drizzle on this salad. It adds the perfect balance of sweetness and tanginess to complement the savory seasoned chicken. And if you ever get the chance to try salsa on your salad . . . trust me, it's worth a shot. —J

For the salad

1 rotisserie chicken, shredded (about 2½ cups)

¼ cup lime juice

½ (1-ounce) packet taco seasoning

3 cups chopped romaine lettuce

1 cup black beans, drained and rinsed

1 cup corn kernels (fresh, frozen and thawed, or canned and drained)

2 cups grape tomatoes, halved

1 avocado, sliced

½ cup finely chopped red onion

½ cup chopped cilantro

For the dressing

¼ cup extra-virgin olive oil

2 tablespoons lime juice

1 tablespoon honey

½ (1-ounce) packet taco seasoning

1 teaspoon minced garlic

Tortilla strips or crushed tortilla chips, for garnish

1 **Make the salad:** In a medium bowl, season the shredded chicken with the lime juice and taco seasoning. Toss together until the chicken is coated. Set aside to marinate for a few minutes while you prepare the rest of the salad.

2 In a large salad bowl, toss together the romaine, black beans, corn, tomatoes, avocado, red onion, and cilantro. Add the seasoned shredded chicken and toss again to combine.

3 **Make the dressing:** In a small bowl, whisk together the olive oil, lime juice, honey, taco seasoning, and garlic until well combined.

4 Drizzle the dressing over the salad and toss everything together. Serve chilled or at room temperature, topping the salad with tortilla strips or crushed tortilla chips for added texture and crunch just before eating.

Make this!

To make your own taco seasoning, combine 2½ teaspoons chili powder, 1½ teaspoons cumin, ½ teaspoon paprika, ½ teaspoon oregano, 1 teaspoon freshly ground black pepper, and 1 teaspoon salt.

TEX-MEX QUESO

We love this dip. Before we knew each other, both of us made a version of it at home and ordered it whenever we saw it on a restaurant menu. And when we started dating and realized that we both love it so much, it was kind of a bonding moment. Our homemade version uses all natural ingredients. If you're a fellow Tex-Mex queso lover, you've got to try this slightly spicy twist on the classic dip. —**A and J**

2 tablespoons butter

½ medium yellow onion, diced

2 jalapeños, seeded and diced

3 garlic cloves, minced

1 teaspoon ground cumin

½ teaspoon onion powder

1 teaspoon salt

½ teaspoon freshly ground black pepper

1 (14-ounce) can diced fire-roasted tomatoes

1 (4-ounce) can diced green chiles

1 (12-ounce) can evaporated milk

3 tablespoons cornstarch

1 cup low-sodium chicken broth

½ pound yellow sharp cheddar cheese, freshly grated

½ pound Monterey Jack cheese, freshly grated

2 ounces cream cheese, softened

2 tablespoons chopped fresh cilantro

Tortilla chips or vegetables, for serving

1 In a large skillet, melt the butter over medium heat. Add the onion and jalapeños and sauté for 4 to 5 minutes, until soft. Add the garlic, cumin, and onion powder and sauté for another minute, until fragrant. Season with the salt and pepper. Stir in the tomatoes and green chiles and cook for an additional 3 to 4 minutes, stirring occasionally.

2 In a small bowl, whisk together the evaporated milk and cornstarch. Stir into the skillet along with the chicken broth. Bring to a boil, reduce to a simmer, and cook for 5 to 6 minutes, stirring occasionally, until the mixture thickens. Stir in the cheddar cheese, Monterey Jack cheese, and cream cheese and mix until melted. Stir in the cilantro until combined. Serve immediately with tortilla chips or your favorite dipping vegetables.

Make this!

You can keep the queso in a slow cooker on the "warm" setting to keep the dip perfectly melted.

BUFFALO CHICKEN DIP

True story: In high school my friend Eric and I started a buffalo wings club. We met every week at Woody's Wings and Things and—you guessed it—ate wings. By the time we graduated, we had twelve members! Even now, at restaurants, I ask for a side of wing sauce to dip my fries (or anything else) into. That's how much I love buffalo sauce. My brother-in-law introduced me to buffalo chicken dip, which was a game changer. It kind of makes me want to bring back our old club meetings again. Eric, get ready! —**J**

8 ounces cream cheese, softened

½ cup ranch dressing

½ cup cayenne pepper sauce (we like Frank's RedHot)

1½ cups shredded Mexican cheese blend, divided

1 rotisserie chicken, shredded (about 2½ cups)

¼ cup blue cheese crumbles, for garnish (optional)

Sliced green onion

Vegetables, tortilla chips, and/or bread, for dipping

1 Preheat the oven to 350°F. Grease an 8-inch-square baking dish with nonstick spray or cooking spray. Set aside.

2 In a large bowl, combine the cream cheese, ranch dressing, cayenne pepper sauce, and 1 cup of Mexican cheese blend. Stir until smooth and mostly free of lumps. Fold in the shredded chicken until evenly distributed.

3 Transfer the mixture to the prepared baking dish and sprinkle the remaining ½ cup of Mexican cheese blend over the top. Bake in the oven for 20 to 25 minutes, until the cheese bubbles and turns slightly golden. Remove from the oven and stir. Garnish with the blue cheese crumbles, if desired, and green onion. Serve with your favorite dippers!

CAPRESE PASTA SALAD

This little dish captures the essence of a classic Italian caprese salad with a fresh, vibrant twist. Each bite has a hint of tangy balsamic vinaigrette, juicy tomatoes, creamy mozzarella, and fragrant basil leaves. Whether enjoyed at a summer picnic or as a quick and easy lunch option, this pasta salad will transport you to Italy without your having to leave your own backyard.

2 cups cherry tomatoes, halved

8 ounces fresh mozzarella pearls

3 tablespoons balsamic vinegar

2 garlic cloves, minced

1 tablespoon drained capers

1 teaspoon salt

½ teaspoon pepper

¼ cup extra-virgin olive oil, plus more for drizzling

12 ounces orecchiette

½ cup fresh basil leaves, torn

1 In a medium bowl, combine the tomatoes and mozzarella. Set aside.

2 In a small bowl, whisk together the balsamic vinegar, garlic, capers, salt, and pepper. Whisk in the olive oil until emulsified. Pour three quarters of the dressing over the tomato and mozzarella mixture and stir until well coated. Allow to marinate for 30 minutes.

3 Bring a large pot of salted water to a boil. Cook the pasta al dente as directed on the package. Drain the pasta and transfer it to a large bowl. Toss with some olive oil and cool to room temperature.

4 Toss the tomato and mozzarella mixture with the cooled pasta and reserved dressing. Fold in the fresh basil leaves.

Crunchy NOODLE CHICKEN SALAD

My first job when I moved to Los Angeles was at Chin Chin restaurant on Sunset Boulevard. The menu there is described as modern Chinese cuisine. The waitstaff got to eat one meal free per day, and my pick almost every time was the chicken salad. I asked Josh if we could make it at home, and he came up with this easy, tasty version! —**A**

For the dressing

3 tablespoons low-sodium soy sauce

2 tablespoons rice vinegar

1 tablespoon sesame oil

1 tablespoon canola oil

1 teaspoon brown sugar

2 teaspoons minced ginger

1 garlic clove, minced

½ teaspoon ground white pepper

For the salad

4 cups finely shredded romaine lettuce

1½ cups finely shredded red cabbage

1 cup shredded carrots

3 green onions, thinly sliced

1 rotisserie chicken, shredded (about 2½ cups)

1 cup crunchy chow mein noodles, for topping

2 teaspoons sesame seeds, for topping

¼ cup sliced almonds, for topping

1 **Make the dressing:** In a mason jar or medium bowl, combine the soy sauce, rice vinegar, sesame oil, canola oil, brown sugar, ginger, garlic, and pepper. Whisk or shake until well blended.

2 **Make the salad:** In a large salad bowl, mix the romaine, cabbage, carrots, green onions, and chicken. Drizzle the dressing over the salad and toss well. Sprinkle the chow mein noodles, sesame seeds, and almonds over the top for some extra crunch.

ESQUITES

Esquites are a mix of elote, a popular Mexican street corn dish, with jalapeño, cotija cheese, and sunflower seeds. Ange and I first encountered this dish on a date night, and I knew from the first bite that I would have to recreate this dish for us at home. You can serve it as an appetizer or a side dish to your main meal. So when you can't get a sitter, enjoy this date night dish at home! —J

2 tablespoons canola oil

6 cups fresh corn, cut from the cob (from about 8 ears)

½ cup raw sunflower seeds, shelled

1 jalapeño pepper, seeded and diced

1 teaspoon minced garlic

⅓ cup Mexican crema or sour cream

⅓ cup mayonnaise

2 tablespoons chopped fresh cilantro, plus more for garnish

2 tablespoons lime juice

¼ cup cotija cheese, crumbled, plus more for garnish

1 teaspoon salt

1 teaspoon freshly ground black pepper

Chipotle or chili powder, for sprinkling

Tortilla chips and lime wedges, for serving

1 In a large skillet, heat the oil over medium-high heat until shimmering. Add the corn, sunflower seeds, and jalapeño to the skillet and cook, stirring, until lightly charred, about 5 minutes. Reduce the heat to medium low and continue cooking for another 5 to 7 minutes, until the sunflower seeds brown and the jalapeño softens. Stir in the garlic and cook for about 1 minute, until fragrant. Remove from heat.

2 In a large bowl, combine the crema or sour cream, mayonnaise, cilantro, lime juice, and cotija cheese. Season with the salt and pepper. Stir until well incorporated and set aside ¼ cup of the mixture in a smaller bowl.

3 Add the corn mixture to the sauce and toss until evenly coated. Transfer to a serving dish and garnish with some additional cilantro, cotija cheese, and a sprinkle of chipotle or chili powder. Drizzle with the reserved crema mixture. Serve with tortilla chips and lime wedges. This dish can be enjoyed warm or cold.

Make this!

If cotija cheese isn't available, you can use crumbled feta or grated Parmesan.

DATE NIGHT!

Spicy PIZZA DIP

Whether it's game day or a chill movie night, this dip is always a crowd pleaser. Pro tip: Serve it with some garlic knots and soft pretzel bread— but be warned, it'll be gone before you know it!

8 ounces cream cheese, softened

1 cup shredded Parmesan, divided

1 tablespoon Italian seasoning

1 cup shredded mozzarella

1 cup marinara or pizza sauce

¼ green bell pepper, seeded and diced

10 to 12 pepperoni slices

½ jalapeño, seeded and sliced (optional)

1 teaspoon red pepper flakes (optional)

Fresh basil leaves, torn, for garnish

Bread, chips, or veggies, for dipping

1 Preheat your oven to 350°F. Grease a 9-inch pie plate with nonstick spray or cooking spray. Set aside.

2 In a medium bowl, mix the cream cheese with ½ cup of Parmesan and the Italian seasoning until well combined.

3 Spread the cream cheese mixture evenly across the bottom of the prepared pie plate. Layer half the mozzarella over the cream cheese, followed by a layer of marinera or pizza sauce. Sprinkle the remaining Parmesan and mozzarella cheeses on top, creating another cheesy layer. Top with the bell pepper and pepperoni, plus the jalapeño and red pepper flakes for extra heat, if desired.

4 Bake for 15 to 18 minutes, until the cheese is bubbling and golden brown and the pepperoni slices are crispy. Garnish with fresh basil leaves. Serve with bread, chips, or veggies.

66 This DIP is always a CROWD-PLEASER.

Turkey CHEESEBURGER DIP

While this cookbook has plenty of ground turkey recipes, this dip is one of my favorites. It has all the traditional burger flavors— onion, cheese, ketchup, mustard, black pepper—but is lighter than a whole burger. Give it a try and thank me later! —**J**

1 tablespoon extra-virgin olive oil

1 pound ground turkey

¼ cup chopped green onions, plus 2 tablespoons for garnish

1 teaspoon onion powder

1 teaspoon garlic powder

1 teaspoon salt

1 teaspoon freshly ground black pepper

1 (14.5-ounce) can diced tomatoes

1 (4-ounce) can diced green chiles

4 ounces cream cheese, softened

1 (5-ounce) can evaporated milk

2 cups shredded cheddar cheese

2 tablespoons yellow mustard

2 tablespoons cayenne pepper sauce (such as Frank's RedHot)

Chips, crackers, bread, and/or veggies, for dipping

1 In a large skillet, heat the olive oil over medium-high heat until shimmering. Add the ground turkey and the ¼ cup chopped green onions to the skillet, and cook, breaking up the meat with a wooden spoon until browned, about 5 minutes. Add the onion powder, garlic powder, salt, and pepper. Reduce heat to medium and stir in the tomatoes and green chiles. Add the cream cheese and evaporated milk to the skillet, stirring continuously, until the cream cheese is fully melted and the mixture is well combined. Continue to cook the mixture for about 3 minutes, stirring, until thickened.

2 Remove the skillet from heat and stir in the cheddar cheese, mustard, and cayenne pepper sauce. Stir until the cheese melts thoroughly and the sauce is creamy. Scoop the mixture into a serving dish or serve in the skillet for a rustic look. Garnish with the 2 tablespoons green onion and serve warm with chips, crackers, bread, and/or veggies.

Fritos
CHILI PIE

The big summer event in my hometown of Archer City, Texas, is the rodeo! For three nights in June, our little town is abuzz with excitement. My dad would get our family front-row seats to watch the action. For years my sister Billie sang the national anthem, and my brother-in-law, my nephews, and I rode in the Grand Entry. Can you tell that this was a big deal in my family? The best item on the rodeo concession stand menu? Fritos Chili Pie! Josh finally got to try it when one of our favorite restaurants offered it as an appetizer. He immediately loved it and created a version we enjoy with friends at home on our back porch. It's like having a little piece of my hometown here in Los Angeles. —**A**

1 tablespoon extra-virgin olive oil

1 pound ground beef

½ medium white onion, diced

1 green bell pepper, seeded and diced

3 garlic cloves, minced

2 tablespoons chili powder

1 teaspoon ground cumin

1 teaspoon dried oregano

1 teaspoon cayenne

1 teaspoon salt

1 teaspoon freshly ground black pepper

2 tablespoons tomato paste

1 (28-ounce) can petite diced tomatoes

1 (15-ounce) can red kidney beans, drained and rinsed

½ cup chicken broth

1 (4-ounce) can green chiles

8 (1-ounce) Fritos bags, for serving

Shredded cheddar cheese, diced white onion, sliced jalapeños, sliced green onions, diced red peppers, and sour cream, for serving

1 In a large, deep skillet, heat the olive oil over medium heat. When the oil is hot and shimmering, add the beef and cook for 4 to 5 minutes, until browned. Add the onion and bell pepper and cook, stirring, until soft, 5 to 6 minutes. Add the garlic and cook until fragrant, about 1 minute. Stir in the chili powder, cumin, oregano, and cayenne and season with the salt and pepper. Cook, stirring, 1 to 2 minutes to toast the spices. Stir in the tomato paste, ensuring that the mixture is well coated. Stir in the diced tomatoes, kidney beans, chicken broth, and chiles. Bring to a boil, then reduce heat to medium low, cover, and simmer for 25 to 30 minutes, stirring occasionally.

2 Carefully cut open one side of a Fritos bag. Add ½ cup of chili to each bag on top of the Fritos. Top as desired with the cheddar cheese, onion, jalapeños, green onions, red peppers, and sour cream.

Make this!

Besides serving in Fritos bags for a fun and casual presentation, this chili is great over rice or baked potatoes or even as a stand-alone dish with a side of cornbread.

Soups and Sides

ITALIAN WEDDING *Soup*

This recipe might just have sealed the deal in our relationship. When we first started dating, we took turns making dinner for each other. When it was my turn, I tried to play it cool, but I was a nervous wreck. I was not a great cook. (Or at least I used to not be until I met Josh. Thanks, babe!) I knew that Josh loved soup, so I scoured the internet, researching people's favorite soup recipes, and that was when I learned about Italian wedding soup. I took it one step at a time and made a few adjustments, knowing Josh's tastes, and OMG, he loved it! It is still his favorite dish that I make. Who knows, maybe you'll find love over soup, too! —**A**

For the meatballs

1 pound ground chicken

½ cup grated Parmesan

⅓ cup plain breadcrumbs

1 large egg, beaten

2 tablespoons Italian seasoning

1 teaspoon salt

½ teaspoon freshly ground black pepper

For the soup

2 tablespoons extra-virgin olive oil

1 medium red onion, diced

6 carrots, peeled and cut into rounds

4 celery ribs, cut into ½-inch pieces

1 teaspoon salt

½ teaspoon freshly ground black pepper

2 garlic cloves, minced

1 cup dry red wine

1 large tomato, seeded and diced

3 cups chopped kale leaves

8 cups chicken broth

2 dried bay leaves

2 (15-ounce) cans cannellini beans, drained and rinsed

1 cup water

1 Make the meatballs: In a large bowl, mix together the ground chicken, Parmesan, breadcrumbs, egg, Italian seasoning, salt, and pepper until well combined. Form into golf ball–size meatballs and set aside on a plate or baking sheet.

2 Make the soup: In a Dutch oven or large soup pot, heat the olive oil over medium heat until shimmering. Add the onion, carrots, and celery and sauté until softened, about 6 to 7 minutes. Season with the salt and pepper and stir in the garlic, cooking until fragrant, about 1 minute.

3 Add the red wine and diced tomato and bring to a simmer. Stir in the kale and cook until wilted, about 2 minutes. Add the chicken broth and bay leaves, bring to a boil, reduce heat to medium low, and simmer, slightly covered, for about 1 hour.

4 Remove the bay leaves and add the cannellini beans and the water. Increase heat to medium and bring to a gentle simmer. Carefully add the meatballs to the soup and cook, covered, until the meatballs are cooked through, 10 to 12 minutes, or until they reach an internal temperature of 165°F. Serve hot.

Honey Sriracha BRUSSELS SPROUTS

Get ready to fall in love with Brussels sprouts all over again—or maybe for the first time! We whip up this side dish at least twice a week because we can't get enough of them, and even our kids are fans! (Parents, you know what a win it is when your kids love a vegetable dish.) The sweetness of honey perfectly balances the kick of sriracha, while the freshly squeezed lemon adds a tangy depth. Trust us, you won't be able to resist this mouthwatering sweet and spicy combo!

1½ pounds Brussels sprouts, trimmed and halved

2 tablespoons extra-virgin olive oil

1 teaspoon salt

½ teaspoon freshly ground black pepper

3 tablespoons honey

2 tablespoons sriracha

⅓ cup lemon juice

1 Preheat your oven to 400°F. Line a large sheet pan with parchment paper. Set aside.

2 Add the Brussels sprouts to a large bowl and drizzle with the olive oil. Toss to coat and season with the salt and pepper. Arrange cut side down in a single layer on the prepared baking sheet. Roast for 45 to 50 minutes, stirring halfway through, until tender and crisp.

3 While the sprouts are roasting, whisk together the honey, sriracha, and lemon juice in a large bowl. Transfer the hot roasted sprouts to the bowl and toss to coat. Serve warm.

Get ready to FALL IN LOVE *with* Brussels Sprouts *all over again!*

Roasted VEGGIE MEDLEY

While many people may assume that I am the only one who bakes and cooks in our relationship, that's not entirely true. Angela has taught me a few things over the years, too, including introducing me to roasted veggies. This veggie medley includes all our favorites on one sheet pan—perfect for a big group dinner or a quick weeknight meal. Thank you, Angela, for teaching me something new and inspiring: this recipe. **—J**

2 medium carrots, peeled and sliced into rounds

½ pound baby potatoes, quartered

1 zucchini, halved and cut into 1-inch pieces

1 yellow squash, halved and cut into 1-inch pieces

1 red or green bell pepper, seeded and cut into 1-inch pieces

1 medium red onion, roughly chopped

2 garlic cloves, minced

3 tablespoons extra-virgin olive oil

2 teaspoon Italian seasoning

½ teaspoon cayenne

2 teaspoons salt

2 teaspoons freshly ground black pepper

Freshly grated Parmesan, for serving

1 Preheat your oven to 400°F. Line a large baking sheet with parchment paper. Set aside.

2 Bring a medium saucepan of salted water to a boil. Add the carrots and potatoes and cook for 5 minutes. Drain in a colander and rinse with cold water. Pat dry.

3 Add the carrots, potatoes, zucchini, yellow squash, bell pepper, onion, and garlic to a large bowl and drizzle with the olive oil. Season with the Italian seasoning, cayenne, salt, and pepper. Toss everything together until well coated and arrange in a single layer on the prepared baking sheet.

4 Roast for 35 to 40 minutes, stirring the vegetables halfway through. Remove from the oven. Sprinkle with Parmesan and serve warm.

Garlic Rosemary SMASHED POTATOES

Sometimes it's tough to choose between the soft, creamy texture of mashed potatoes and the crispy edges of fries. Enter Garlic Rosemary Smashed Potatoes, the best of both worlds!

1½ pounds baby Yukon Gold or baby red potatoes

3 tablespoons extra-virgin olive oil

2 teaspoons garlic powder

2 teaspoons dried rosemary

2 teaspoons salt

1 teaspoon freshly ground black pepper

Freshly grated Parmesan and chopped parsley, for topping

1 Preheat your oven to 425°F. Line a sheet pan with parchment paper. Set aside.

2 Add the potatoes to a pot of cold salted water and bring to a boil. Cook until just tender, about 15 minutes. Drain and cool slightly, then pat dry with a clean kitchen towel or paper towels.

3 Transfer the potatoes to the prepared baking sheet. Gently press each one with the bottom of a glass or a potato masher to about ½ inch thickness.

4 In a small bowl, mix together the olive oil, garlic powder, and rosemary. Drizzle the mixture over the potatoes, tossing to coat. Season with the salt and pepper. Arrange the potatoes in a single, even layer. Roast for 20 to 25 minutes, until golden brown and crispy at the edges. Serve warm, topped with grated Parmesan and chopped parsley.

ISABEL *and* CADE help *with the* groceries

CREAMY CHICKEN *and* *Wild Rice* SOUP

Here's one of Angela's favorite soups! It's packed with tender chicken, nutty wild rice, and fresh veggies in a rich, creamy broth made with a delicious roux. If you can't find a wild rice blend, you can use plain wild rice or even substitute another grain such as brown rice, farro, or barley. Remember that cooking time may vary depending on the grain you choose. —**J**

1 cup wild rice blend

1¾ cups water

1 tablespoon extra-virgin olive oil

6 tablespoons butter

1 medium yellow onion, diced

4 medium carrots, peeled and diced

3 celery ribs, diced

3 garlic cloves, minced

½ teaspoon dried thyme

½ teaspoon dried rosemary

½ teaspoon dried sage

½ teaspoon dried marjoram

½ cup all-purpose flour

6 cups chicken broth

1 teaspoon salt

1 teaspoon freshly ground black pepper

1½ cups whole milk

1 rotisserie chicken, shredded (about 2½ cups)

½ cup sour cream

Chopped parsley, chives, or green onions, for topping

1 To a medium saucepan, add the rice, water, and the olive oil. Stir to combine. Bring the mixture to a boil, then cover and reduce heat to low. Simmer for 35 to 45 minutes, until the water is absorbed and the rice is soft. Remove from heat and set aside.

2 In a Dutch oven or large soup pot, melt the butter over medium heat. Add the onion, carrots, and celery and sauté for 5 to 6 minutes, until soft. Add the garlic, thyme, rosemary, sage, and marjoram and cook for about 1 minute, until the garlic is fragrant. Sprinkle in the flour and cook, stirring, until all the vegetables are evenly coated and the flour is lightly toasted, about 3 minutes. Slowly add the chicken broth, stirring and making sure that there are no lumps of flour. Season with the salt and pepper. Bring the soup to a boil, then cover, reduce heat to medium low, and simmer for 15 to 20 minutes, stirring occasionally, until the vegetables are tender. Stir in the cooked rice, milk, and chicken and cook until the chicken is heated through, about 5 minutes. Remove from heat and stir in the sour cream. Serve hot, topped with chopped parsley, chives, or green onions.

GREEN CHILE ENCHILADA *Soup*

This might just be the easiest soup you'll ever make. With a store-bought rotisserie chicken and premade green enchilada sauce, it comes together fast. Bursting with southwestern flavors, fresh veggies, a generous sprinkle of cheese, and crispy tortilla strips on top, it's a winner every time. Customize it to your family's taste by adding beans (such as black beans or pinto beans) for more protein; adjust the spice level by varying the amount of jalapeño used or by adding a pinch of cayenne pepper for extra heat. For a milder soup, remove the seeds from the jalapeño. —**J**

2 tablespoons extra-virgin olive oil

½ medium red onion, diced

1 jalapeño, diced

4 mini sweet peppers, diced

4 carrots, peeled and cut into rounds

1 teaspoon salt

½ teaspoon freshly ground black pepper

1 rotisserie chicken, shredded (about 2½ cups)

3 cups chicken broth

2 (15-ounce) cans green chile enchilada sauce

1 cup frozen corn

Tortilla strips, shredded cheese blend, and fresh cilantro leaves, for topping

In a large Dutch oven or pot, heat the olive oil over medium heat until shimmering. Add the onion, jalapeño, peppers, and carrots and sauté until soft, 5 to 6 minutes. Season with the salt and pepper. Add the shredded chicken and sauté for about 1 minute. Stir in the chicken broth, enchilada sauce, and frozen corn. Bring to a boil, then reduce to a simmer and cook, partially covered, for 10 to 15 minutes, stirring occasionally. Serve hot, topped with tortilla strips, shredded cheese blend, and cilantro leaves.

66 **This might just be** *the* **EASIEST SOUP** you'll ever make.

Homestyle CHICKEN NOODLE SOUP

As every soup lover knows, a homestyle chicken noodle soup is the ultimate comfort food. It's perfect for warming up on chilly days or nursing yourself back to health when you have a cold. It's simple and soul soothing and will always make you feel good. For this recipe, we love using Grandma's or Reames frozen egg noodles for their texture and flavor, but shelf-stable noodles or homemade noodles are excellent alternatives. —J

3 tablespoons extra-virgin olive oil

1 medium yellow onion, diced

5 carrots, peeled and cut into rounds

5 celery ribs, chopped

3 garlic cloves, minced

1 teaspoon salt

1 teaspoon freshly ground black pepper

8 cups chicken broth

1 tablespoon poultry seasoning

4 to 6 bones from a rotisserie chicken (drumsticks, thighs, and wings)

1 (11-ounce) package frozen homestyle egg noodles

1 rotisserie chicken, shredded (about 2½ cups)

1 tablespoon fresh dill, chopped

2 tablespoons lemon juice

1 tablespoon chopped parsley, for topping

1 In a Dutch oven or large soup pot, heat the olive oil over medium heat until shimmering. Add the onion, carrots, and celery and sauté until soft, 6 to 7 minutes. Stir in the garlic, salt, and pepper and sauté until fragrant, about 1 minute longer.

2 Add the broth, poultry seasoning, and chicken bones and bring to a simmer. Reduce heat to medium low and simmer for 10 to 12 minutes, until the carrots are tender. Add the noodles and cook for 6 to 8 minutes, until al dente, stirring occasionally to help break them apart. Once the noodles are done, remove the chicken bones, stir in the shredded chicken, and cook for about 2 minutes to warm. Stir in the dill and lemon juice. Serve hot, sprinkled with the chopped parsley.

LEMON CHICKEN SOUP *with* TOASTED ORZO

Here's one the whole family loves! Tangy, salty, fresh, and nutty flavors all contained in one colorful bowl filled with delicious vegetables. The orzo adds a wonderful toasty taste that elevates this soup to another level. If you need a great dish to take to a potluck, this is definitely a crowd pleaser.

2 tablespoons butter

¾ cup orzo

2 tablespoons extra-virgin olive oil

2 shallots, finely chopped

2 carrots, peeled and diced

1 red bell pepper, seeded and diced

2 zucchini, diced

2 garlic cloves, minced

1 teaspoon minced ginger

½ teaspoon dried thyme

½ teaspoon dried rosemary

2 teaspoons lemon zest

1 teaspoon salt

1 teaspoon freshly ground black pepper

6 cups chicken broth

1 rotisserie chicken, shredded (about 2½ cups)

½ cup frozen peas

¼ cup finely chopped fresh parsley

¼ cup lemon juice

1 In a Dutch oven or large soup pot, melt the butter over medium heat. Add the orzo and cook, stirring frequently, until toasted, 3 to 4 minutes. Transfer the orzo to a plate and set aside.

2 In the same pot, heat the olive oil over medium heat until shimmering. Add the shallots, carrots, bell pepper, and zucchini, sautéing until soft, 5 to 6 minutes. Stir in the garlic and ginger, cooking until fragrant, about 1 minute. Stir in the thyme, rosemary, lemon zest, salt, and pepper. Return the orzo to the pot and pour in the chicken broth. Increase heat to medium high, bring the mixture to a boil, reduce heat to a simmer, and cook until the orzo is tender, roughly 5 minutes. Lower heat to medium low and add the chicken and peas. Cook for just a few more minutes until nice and warm. Remove from heat and stir in the parsley and lemon juice. Serve hot.

Make this!

Browning the orzo is essential, as it adds a nutty flavor to the dish. Stir it constantly to ensure even browning and prevent burning.

PASTA E FAGIOLI

In high school, I worked a few nights a week at Olive Garden, first as a host and then as a server. I had never heard of pasta e fagioli before working there, but after just one bite, I was hooked. This hearty soup, packed with white and red beans, ground beef, fresh tomatoes, and tube-shaped pasta in a savory broth, feels like an Italian version of chili. —**J**

2 tablespoons extra-virgin olive oil, divided

1 pound Italian sausage, casings removed

1 medium yellow onion, diced

3 carrots, peeled and diced

2 celery ribs, diced

2 garlic cloves, minced

1 teaspoon salt

½ teaspoon freshly ground black pepper

1 (14.5-ounce) can diced fire-roasted tomatoes

2 tablespoons tomato paste

4 cups chicken broth

1 (15-ounce) can red kidney beans, drained and rinsed

1 (15-ounce) can cannellini beans, drained and rinsed

1½ cups tube-shaped pasta such as ditalini, tubettini, or elbow pasta

1 tablespoon apple cider vinegar or lemon juice

Chopped parsley and freshly grated Parmesan, for topping

1 In a large Dutch oven or soup pot, heat 1 tablespoon olive oil over medium-high heat until shimmering. Add the sausage and cook, breaking apart with a wooden spoon, until browned, 5 to 6 minutes. Remove with a slotted spoon to a plate lined with paper towels and set aside.

2 Reduce heat to medium and add the remaining tablespoon of olive oil. Add the onion, carrots, and celery and cook for 4 to 5 minutes, until tender. Stir in the garlic and cook until fragrant, about 1 minute. Season with the salt and pepper. Stir in the tomatoes and tomato paste, stirring to coat all the vegetables. Add the chicken broth, kidney beans, and cannellini beans, increase heat to medium high, and bring the soup to a boil. Reduce heat to medium low, cover, and simmer lightly for 15 to 20 minutes, until the vegetables are tender.

3 While the soup is simmering, cook the pasta in a pot of boiling salted water according to the package instructions until al dente. Drain and toss with a little olive oil to prevent sticking.

4 Stir the cooked pasta and the browned sausage into the soup. Remove the pot from heat and stir in the apple cider vinegar or lemon juice. Serve hot, sprinkled with chopped parsley and grated Parmesan.

POTATOES *au Gratin* with CARAMELIZED ONION

When you're craving something that's both comforting and a bit fancy, this hearty side dish is the answer! Layers of thinly sliced potatoes mingle with sweet, golden caramelized onion, all covered in creamy, cheesy goodness. Tip: Make it in a skillet to give an extra touch of crispiness to the outer layer while keeping layers of melt-in-your-mouth flavor in the middle.

2½ pounds Yukon Gold potatoes, peeled and sliced ⅛ inch thick

3 tablespoons butter, divided

1 medium yellow onion, thinly sliced

¼ cup white wine

2 teaspoons minced garlic

1 tablespoon fresh thyme, minced

1 teaspoon salt

1 teaspoon freshly ground black pepper

2 cups heavy cream

1 cup grated sharp cheddar cheese

1 cup grated Gruyère

Freshly chopped chives or sprigs of thyme, for garnish

1 Preheat your oven to 350°F. Grease an 11-by-7-inch baking dish or a 12-inch cast-iron skillet with cooking spray or olive oil. Set aside.

2 Submerge the sliced potatoes in a bowl of cold water to prevent discoloration and remove excess starch. Set aside.

3 In a medium skillet, melt 1 tablespoon of butter over medium heat. Add the onion slices and cook, stirring, for about 15 minutes, until they are a nice golden color. Deglaze the skillet with the white wine, allowing the onion to absorb the flavors as the liquid reduces, and cook until just dry. Remove from heat.

4 In a medium saucepan, melt the remaining 2 tablespoons of butter over medium heat. Add the garlic, sautéing until just fragrant. Add the thyme, salt, and pepper.

5 Pour in the cream, stirring continuously, and allow the mixture to simmer gently until it thickens, about 5 minutes. Remove from heat and stir in the grated cheddar until it's completely melted and the sauce is smooth.

6 Drain the potato slices well and pat them dry. Layer the potatoes at the bottom of the prepared baking dish or skillet, overlapping the slices slightly for a shingled effect. When you have completely covered the bottom of the dish or skillet, add a layer of caramelized onion over the potato layer and pour a portion of the cream sauce over the top. Continue layering in this fashion, finishing with a layer of potatoes and cream sauce.

7 Bake for 55 minutes to 1 hour 5 minutes, until the gratin is bubbling around the edges and golden brown on top and the potatoes are tender.

8 Switch the broiler on. Finish by sprinkling the grated Gruyère on top of the potatoes. Briefly broil for a beautiful browned, melty, bubbly crust. Remove from the oven and let the gratin rest and set for 15 to 20 minutes before serving. Garnish with freshly chopped chives or sprigs of thyme.

Lemon Dill
CHICKEN
MEATBALL SOUP

You might be wondering "Why does Josh have so many recipes for meatball soup?" Honestly, I had to whittle down the number I wanted to include! Variations on meatball soup are some of my all-time favorites; they hit all the right notes for a hearty, balanced meal while bursting with flavor. This dill and lemon combo is fantastic, and when you add farro, you get an incredible texture that's out of this world. —**J**

For the meatballs

1 pound ground chicken

⅓ cup plain breadcrumbs

1 large egg, beaten

¼ cup fresh dill, finely chopped

2 teaspoons lemon zest

½ teaspoon salt

½ teaspoon freshly ground black pepper

For the soup

1 cup farro

2 tablespoons extra-virgin olive oil

1 medium yellow onion, diced

3 carrots, peeled and cut into rounds

3 celery ribs, chopped

1 teaspoon salt

1 teaspoon freshly ground black pepper

2 garlic cloves, minced

½ teaspoon dried thyme

½ teaspoon dried rosemary

1 cup white wine

6 cups chicken broth

¼ cup lemon juice

2 teaspoons lemon zest

¼ cup fresh dill, finely chopped

Chopped parsley, for topping

1 **Make the meatballs:** In a large bowl, mix the ground chicken, breadcrumbs, egg, dill, lemon zest, salt, and pepper. Shape the mixture into golf ball–size meatballs and set aside on a dish or baking sheet.

2 **Make the soup:** Cook the farro according to the package instructions. Set aside.

3 In a Dutch oven or large soup pot, heat the olive oil over medium heat until shimmering. Add the onion, carrots, and celery and sauté until soft, about 7 minutes. Season with the salt and pepper. Stir in the garlic, thyme, and rosemary and cook until fragrant, about 1 minute. Add the wine and reduce it until almost dry. Stir in the chicken broth, lemon juice, lemon zest, and dill. Bring to a simmer, reduce heat to low, and cook, uncovered, for 20 minutes, stirring occasionally.

4 Increase heat to medium and bring to a gentle simmer. Carefully add the meatballs to the soup and cook, covered, until the meatballs are cooked through, 10 to 12 minutes or until they reach an internal temperature of 165°F. Stir in the cooked farro. Serve hot, garnished with chopped parsley.

Red Curry TURKEY MEATBALL SOUP

If you love a spicy ramen dish, you will love this soup. Tender seasoned turkey meatballs combine perfectly with fresh veggies and soft rice noodles in a rich and spicy coconut broth. Each spoonful contains a delightful balance of spiciness and creaminess. Ange and I both love this soup with a little spice, but you can season it to your own heat preference. —**J**

For the meatballs

1 pound ground turkey

1 large egg

½ cup panko breadcrumbs

3 green onions, finely chopped

2 garlic cloves, minced

1 teaspoon minced ginger

2 tablespoons red curry paste

1 tablespoon curry powder

1 tablespoon soy sauce

Noodles and things

1 red bell pepper, seeded and sliced into small strips

6 ounces sugar snap peas, stringless

2 cups bean sprouts

6 ounces rice stick noodles

1 teaspoon coconut oil

For the broth

1 tablespoon coconut oil

2 garlic cloves, minced

1 teaspoon minced ginger

2 teaspoons red curry paste

1 tablespoon curry powder

1 cup unsweetened coconut milk

2 cups chicken broth

¼ cup fresh lime juice

1 teaspoon soy sauce

1 teaspoon salt

Chopped fresh basil, sliced green onions, and crushed peanuts, for topping

1 Make the meatballs: Preheat your oven to 400°F. Line a rimmed baking sheet with parchment paper.

2 In a large bowl, combine the turkey, egg, breadcrumbs, green onions, garlic, ginger, red curry paste, curry powder, and soy sauce. Make walnut-size meatballs using a spoon or a small scoop. Place on the prepared baking sheet. You should have about 24 small meatballs. Bake for 20 to 25 minutes or until they reach an internal temperature of 165°F, turning halfway through.

3 Prepare the noodles and things: Bring a medium pot of salted water to a boil. Add the bell pepper, peas, and bean sprouts to the water and cook until just tender, about 3 minutes. Remove from the pot using a slotted spoon and set aside. Cook the rice noodles in the same pot of boiling water for 3 minutes. Drain well and return to the pot along with the coconut oil. Toss together and set aside.

4 Make the broth: In a medium saucepan, cook the coconut oil, garlic, and ginger over medium heat for about 1 minute, until the garlic is fragrant. Stir in the red curry paste and curry powder, then add the coconut milk, chicken broth, lime juice, soy sauce, and salt. Bring to a boil, reduce heat to a simmer, and cook for 5 minutes.

5 Finish the soup: Divide the noodles among the bowls and top with the bell pepper, snap peas, sprouts, and meatballs. Ladle broth into each bowl. Serve hot, topped with chopped basil, sliced green onions, and crushed peanuts.

Make this!

To make your own curry spice blend, combine 2 teaspoons paprika, 1 teaspoon turmeric, ½ teaspoon ground coriander, ½ teaspoon dry mustard, ½ teaspoon ground ginger, ½ teaspoon ground cumin, ½ teaspoon freshly ground black pepper, ¼ teaspoon ground white pepper, and ¼ teaspoon cayenne.

SMOKED SAUSAGE *and* CABBAGE SOUP

Growing up, I was not a fan of cabbage. It always seemed like a bland, less appealing version of lettuce that somehow found its way to the dinner table too often. But everything changed when I discovered this soup. The bitterness of the cabbage is perfectly balanced by the savory, smoky notes of the sausage, making for a rich and comforting soup. Trust me, this soup will make you see cabbage in a whole new light! —**J**

3 tablespoons extra-virgin olive oil, divided

16 ounces smoked kielbasa sausage, cut into rounds

1 medium yellow onion, diced

3 carrots, peeled and cut into rounds

3 celery ribs, chopped

2 garlic cloves, minced

1 teaspoon salt

1 teaspoon freshly ground black pepper

1 small green cabbage, chopped into bite-size pieces

1 cup dry red wine

4 cups beef broth

1 (14.5-ounce) can diced fire-roasted tomatoes

1 pound red potatoes, diced

2 tablespoons Italian seasoning

Chopped parsley, for garnish

1 In a Dutch oven or a large soup pot, heat 1 tablespoon of olive oil over medium heat until shimmering. Add the sausage and cook for 4 to 5 minutes, until lightly browned. Remove the sausage from the pot and set aside on a plate.

2 Turn the heat to medium high, add the remaining 2 tablespoons of olive oil, followed by the onion, carrots, and celery, and sauté until soft, 5 to 7 minutes. Add the minced garlic and cook for about 1 minute, just until fragrant. Season with the salt and pepper. Add the cabbage to the pot and cook for about 2 minutes, until it starts to wilt. Pour in the red wine, stirring and letting it reduce for about 2 minutes. Add the broth, tomatoes, potatoes, browned sausage, and Italian seasoning and stir to combine. Bring to a boil, reduce heat to a simmer, and cook, covered, for about 25 minutes, until the potatoes are tender and can be pierced easily with a fork. Serve hot, sprinkled with chopped parsley.

Southwest WHITE CHICKEN CHILI

When you think of chili, you might picture red beans, tomatoes, and ground beef, right? Well, let me introduce you to a new family favorite. This dish is a fresher, lighter take on chili that's incredibly versatile and easy on the stomach. If you desire a milder chili, opt for mild canned green chilies. For a spicier kick, look for hot chili varieties or even add a diced jalapeño or two. —**J**

2 tablespoons extra-virgin olive oil

1 medium white onion, diced

2 garlic cloves, minced

1 teaspoon salt

½ teaspoon freshly ground black pepper

1 (1-ounce) packet taco seasoning

2 (4-ounce) cans diced green chiles

4 cups chicken broth

4 cups shredded Mexican cheese blend

1 cup fresh or frozen corn

2 (15-ounce) cans cannellini beans, drained and rinsed

1 rotisserie chicken, shredded (about 2½ cups)

2 tablespoons lime juice

2 tablespoons fresh cilantro, chopped

1 cup sour cream

Shredded cheddar cheese, chopped fresh cilantro, sliced avocado, and tortilla chips, for topping

1 In a large pot or Dutch oven, heat the olive oil over medium heat until shimmering. Sauté the onion until tender, about 4 to 5 minutes. Add the garlic and cook until fragrant, about 1 minute. Season with the salt and pepper. Stir in the taco seasoning, green chiles, and chicken broth. Bring to a boil over medium-high heat, then reduce heat to medium low and simmer lightly, stirring occasionally, for about 20 minutes, until the broth is reduced slightly.

2 Reduce heat to low and add the cheese by handfuls, stirring, until smooth and melted. Add the corn and beans and increase heat to medium low. Simmer for about 5 minutes, until the cheese is completely melted and the sauce thickens even more. Add the shredded chicken, lime juice, and cilantro, cooking until the chicken is thoroughly heated, about 2 minutes.

3 Remove from heat, fold in the sour cream, and let stand for 5 minutes to thicken. Serve hot in bowls, topped with shredded cheese, chopped fresh cilantro, sliced avocado, and tortilla chips.

Make this!

To make your own taco seasoning, combine 2½ teaspoons chili powder, 1½ teaspoons cumin, ½ teaspoon paprika, ½ teaspoon oregano, 1 teaspoon freshly ground black pepper, and 1 teaspoon salt.

SPICY CREAMED CORN

Creamed corn has a reputation for being a bit … well … uninspiring. But this isn't the creamed corn of your childhood! I put a fresh spin on this classic sweet and buttery side dish by adding a little kick with jalapeños and green chiles. It's got that rich, creamy texture everyone loves, plus a pop of flavor that makes it a hit at summer cookouts and holiday dinners alike. —**J**

2 tablespoons butter

½ medium yellow onion, diced

½ red bell pepper, seeded and diced

1 jalapeño, seeded and diced

2 garlic cloves, minced

1 teaspoon salt

1 teaspoon freshly ground black pepper

4 cups frozen corn, thawed

1 (10-ounce) can diced tomatoes with green chiles, drained

2 tablespoons all-purpose flour

1½ cups milk (2% or whole)

1 teaspoon sugar

1 teaspoon smoked paprika

¼ cup freshly grated Parmesan

Chopped fresh cilantro, for topping

1 In a large skillet, melt the butter over medium heat. Add the onion, bell pepper, and jalapeño to the skillet. Sauté until the vegetables are soft, 4 to 5 minutes.

2 Add the garlic and cook for another minute, until fragrant. Season with the salt and pepper. Stir in the corn and tomatoes and cook for 2 to 3 minutes.

3 Sprinkle the flour over the vegetable mixture, stirring well to coat. Cook, stirring, for 1 to 2 minutes, ensuring that the flour is fully incorporated with the vegetables. Slowly pour in the milk, stirring constantly to prevent lumps from forming. Bring the mixture to a gentle simmer over medium-high heat, then reduce heat to low. Simmer gently for 10 to 12 minutes, stirring occasionally, until the mixture has thickened. Taste for seasoning and sprinkle in the sugar and smoked paprika.

4 Remove from heat and stir in the grated Parmesan. Serve warm, sprinkled with chopped fresh cilantro.

Make this!

To make your own taco seasoning, combine 2½ teaspoons chili powder, 1½ teaspoons cumin, ½ teaspoon paprika, ½ teaspoon oregano, 1 teaspoon freshly ground black pepper, and 1 teaspoon salt.

TACO SOUP

If you asked me to list our favorite regular family meals, taco night would always be at the top of my ranking. But sometimes it's fun to mix things up a bit. Josh created this taco soup, and I loved it and told him it had to be in our book! Imagine all the bold, zesty flavors of your favorite tacos but served up in a warm, comforting broth. This taco soup is so delicious and satisfying, you'll find yourself going back for seconds (and maybe thirds). —A

2 tablespoons extra-virgin olive oil, divided

1 pound ground beef

1 medium white onion, diced

1 green bell pepper, seeded and diced

1 red bell pepper, seeded and diced

1 jalapeño, seeded and diced

2 garlic cloves, minced

1 teaspoon salt

½ teaspoon freshly ground black pepper

1 (1-ounce) packet taco seasoning

6 cups chicken or beef broth

2 (14-ounce) cans fire-roasted diced tomatoes

2 (4-ounce) cans green chiles

1½ cups frozen corn

2 (14.5-ounce) cans black beans, drained and rinsed

¼ cup fresh cilantro, chopped

2 tablespoons lime juice

Sliced green onion, shredded cheddar cheese, sour cream, and tortilla strips, for topping

1 In a Dutch oven or large soup pot, heat 1 tablespoon of olive oil over medium heat until shimmering. Add the ground beef and sauté, breaking up with a wooden spoon, until browned, 5 to 6 minutes. Using a slotted spoon, transfer the beef to a plate and drain off any excess grease from the pot.

2 Place the pot back on the heat and add the onion, bell peppers, and jalapeño. Sauté until tender, 4 to 6 minutes. Stir in the garlic, cooking it just until fragrant, about 1 minute. Season with the salt and pepper. Return the browned beef to the pot along with any drippings and add the taco seasoning, stirring well to ensure that the meat is thoroughly coated with the spices. Stir in the broth, tomatoes, green chiles, corn, and black beans. Bring to a gentle boil, reduce heat, and simmer, covered, for 30 minutes, stirring occasionally. Remove from heat and stir in the cilantro and lime juice. Serve hot, topped with sliced green onion, shredded cheddar cheese, sour cream, and tortilla strips.

Make this!

To make your own taco seasoning, combine 2½ teaspoons chili powder, 1½ teaspoons cumin, ½ teaspoon paprika, ½ teaspoon oregano, 1 teaspoon freshly ground black pepper, and 1 teaspoon salt.

SPINACH TORTELLINI SOUP *with* ITALIAN SAUSAGE

I have no idea who came up with the brilliant idea of cheese tortellini, but let me just say thank you! Tortellini is the star of this soup, complemented by the tangy tomato broth that provides just the right hint of spice. It strikes the perfect balance between hearty and light. —**J**

1 tablespoon extra-virgin olive oil

1 pound Italian sausage, casings removed

½ medium yellow onion, diced

2 garlic cloves, minced

5 fresh basil leaves, torn into small pieces

1 teaspoon salt

1 teaspoon freshly ground black pepper

1 (14.5-ounce) can diced fire-roasted tomatoes

2 teaspoons Italian seasoning

6 cups chicken broth

1 (9-ounce) package cheese tortellini

6 cups baby spinach

¼ cup lemon juice

Parmesan and torn fresh basil leaves, for topping

In a Dutch oven or large soup pot, heat the olive oil over medium heat until shimmering. Add the sausage and onion, and cook, stirring and breaking up the sausage with a wooden spoon, until the sausage is browned and the onion is tender, 6 to 7 minutes. Toss in the garlic and basil and sauté until fragrant, about 1 minute longer. Season with the salt and pepper. Stir in the tomatoes, Italian seasoning, and chicken broth and bring to a gentle boil over medium heat. Add the tortellini and cook until tender, 5 to 6 minutes. Remove from heat and add the spinach by handfuls, stirring, until wilted, about 1 minute. Stir in the lemon juice. Serve hot topped with grated Parmesan and torn fresh basil leaves.

BEEF *with* VEGETABLES *and* BARLEY SOUP

During the school year over the colder months in Colorado, my mom would pack me a thermos full of Campbell's beef with vegetables & barley soup. While my friends were eating boring sandwiches or trading snacks, I was happily unscrewing the cap of my Transformers thermos to eat my soup. It warmed me up from the inside out and made even the gloomiest days feel cozy. Years later, when I started cooking for myself, I knew I would have to make a homemade version. The tender veggies, savory chunks of beef, hearty barley, and rich broth are made even better by the fact that it's crafted from scratch. **–J**

1½ **pounds chuck roast or beef stew meat, cut into ½-inch cubes**

2 teaspoons salt, divided

1 teaspoon freshly ground black pepper, divided

2 tablespoons extra-virgin olive oil

4 carrots, peeled and sliced into rounds

4 celery ribs, cut into ½-inch pieces

3 garlic cloves, minced

1 cup dry red wine

2 tablespoons Worcestershire sauce

2 tablespoons Italian seasoning

1 cup tomato juice

1 cup pearl onions, peeled

1 cup frozen peas

1 cup frozen corn

6 cups beef broth

⅔ **cup barley**

1½ **cups red potatoes, cut into ½-inch pieces**

Chopped parsley, for topping

1 Season the beef with half the salt and pepper.

2 In a Dutch oven or large soup pot, heat the olive oil over medium-high heat until shimmering. Sear the beef until browned on all sides, working in batches, if needed. Transfer to a bowl and reserve.

3 Add the carrots and celery to the pot, and sauté for 5 to 6 minutes, until they soften and lightly caramelize. Stir in the garlic and season with the remaining salt and pepper. Cook, stirring, for about 1 minute. Add the red wine and use the back of a wooden spoon to scrape up any browned bits on the bottom of the pot. Add the Worcestershire sauce and Italian seasoning. Cook for about 2 minutes to allow the wine to reduce and the flavors to meld. Return the beef to the pot and add the tomato juice, pearl onions, peas, and corn. Stir together and cook for 2 minutes. Add the broth, barley, and potatoes and stir to combine. Bring to a boil, reduce heat to a simmer, cover, and cook for 40 to 45 minutes, until the beef is tender. Serve hot, sprinkled with chopped parsley.

Dinners

SKILLET-ROASTED CHICKEN *with Rosemary Lemon Pan Sauce*

This dish is one of my favorites and always makes me feel like a pro in the kitchen. I love deglazing the pan with wine, reducing it to perfection, sautéing garlic until it's just right, chopping fresh rosemary, and finishing it off with a splash of lemon juice and butter. I always make extra sauce because our kids want to dip everything into it! This sauce pairs wonderfully with pasta. Cook your favorite pasta al dente, toss it with some of the pan sauce, and serve it as a bed for the sliced chicken. Linguine, spaghetti, or fettuccine work well. Despite how fancy it sounds, this recipe is surprisingly simple. You'll feel like a gourmet chef in no time! —J

For the chicken

4 boneless, skinless chicken breasts (about 1½ pounds)

Salt and freshly ground black pepper

2 tablespoons extra-virgin olive oil

For the sauce

3 garlic cloves, minced

2 teaspoons fresh rosemary, minced

1 teaspoon salt

1 teaspoon freshly ground black pepper

¼ cup white wine

1 cup chicken broth

2 tablespoons unsalted butter

2 tablespoons fresh lemon juice

1 **Make the chicken:** Preheat your oven to 375°F.

2 Place the chicken breasts between two pieces of parchment paper or plastic wrap and gently pound them with a meat mallet or rollling pin to an even thickness of about ½ inch. Pat dry with a paper towel.

3 With a steady hand and a sharp knife, cut a diagonal crosshatch pattern about ¼ inch deep into each chicken breast. This will allow the seasoning to penetrate more deeply. Season both sides with salt and pepper.

4 In a large oven-safe skillet, heat the olive oil over high heat. When the oil begins to shimmer slightly, carefully place the chicken in the pan, scored side down. Reduce heat to medium, cook for about 5 minutes, until golden brown, and flip. Move the skillet to the oven and bake for 10 to 12 minutes or until the internal temperature reaches 165°F on an instant-read thermometer. Remove the skillet from the oven and place it back on the stovetop. Place the chicken breasts on a cutting board to rest while you make the pan sauce.

5 **Make the sauce:** Heat the skillet with the drippings over medium heat and sauté the garlic and rosemary for about 1 minute until fragrant. Season with the salt and pepper. Deglaze the skillet with the white wine, cooking until the liquid has almost evaporated and scraping up the brown bits from the pan. Add the chicken broth and bring to a boil. Cook for 3 to 5 minutes, until the sauce is reduced by half. Turn off the heat and stir in the butter and lemon juice until the butter is melted. Slice the chicken against the grain and drizzle with the warm sauce.

CREOLE *Turkey and* SAUSAGE FOIL PACK

Okay, here is a pet peeve of mine: when I ask my family what they want for dinner and they say, "Whatever." I can't grocery shop for "whatever." (Also, "whatever" never actually means whatever.) Enter these foil packs, which come together easily and are perfect for busy evenings when your family members might be eating at different times. Prep them ahead of time, then pop them into the oven—or onto the grill for a smoky flavor—and in no time at all, you have a great dinner! They're ideal for camping. Make a batch, store them in the cooler, and you'll have an easy meal ready to cook over the fire. Experiment with different vegetables; bite-size zucchini, cherry tomatoes, or corn can be great additions or substitutions. —**J**

16 ounces ground turkey

12 ounces smoked turkey sausage, cut into rounds

½ pound baby red potatoes, quartered

1 medium red onion, roughly chopped

1 green bell pepper, roughly chopped

1 cup cherry tomatoes, sliced in half

4 garlic cloves, minced

¼ cup extra-virgin olive oil

2 tablespoons Creole seasoning (such as Tony Chachere's)

1 teaspoon salt

1 teaspoon freshly ground black pepper

Chopped fresh parsley, for topping

1 Preheat the oven to 400°F. Prepare six squares of heavy-duty double-layer aluminum foil, each measuring about 12 by 12 inches.

2 In a large bowl, combine the turkey, sausage, potatoes, onion, bell pepper, tomatoes, and garlic. Drizzle with the olive oil and season with the Creole seasoning, salt, and pepper. Toss together until combined and the turkey is broken up into small pieces. Divide the mixture evenly among the foil squares. Securely wrap the foil squares up to seal.

3 Place the foil packets on a sheet pan and bake in the oven for 40 to 45 minutes, turning them over halfway through. Carefully open each packet and allow the steam to escape. Sprinkle with chopped fresh parsley before serving.

Make this!

To make your own Creole seasoning mix, combine 1½ teaspoons paprika, 1 teaspoon salt, ½ teaspoon cayenne, ½ teaspoon freshly ground black pepper, ½ teaspoon onion powder, ½ teaspoon garlic powder, ½ teaspoon dried oregano, ½ teaspoon dried basil, ¼ teaspoon dried thyme, and ¼ teaspoon ground white pepper.

CHICKEN MILANESE
and Chicken Parmesan

There is one dish all three of our kids can agree on, and it's this one. When they were little, we went to our local neighborhood Italian restaurant, and they fell in love with chicken Milanese. It became the dinner they all wanted for birthdays and any other special occasion. So here is my version of our kids' favorite dinner entrée! For a more delicate crust, try using panko breadcrumbs. For a gluten-free option, crush gluten-free crackers or grind rolled oats and season them with your favorite herbs. —**J**

4 boneless, skinless chicken breasts

⅔ cup all-purpose flour

1 teaspoon salt, plus more as needed

1 teaspoon freshly ground black pepper, plus more as needed

2 large eggs

2 tablespoons milk

1 cup plain breadcrumbs

1 teaspoon Italian seasoning

1 teaspoon garlic powder

Zest of 1 large lemon

½ cup grated Parmesan

¼ cup Extra-virgin olive oil

Chopped parsley and lemon wedges, for serving

1 Place the chicken breasts between two pieces of parchment paper or plastic wrap. Gently pound them with a meat mallet or rolling pin to an even thickness of about ¼ inch. Pat dry with a paper towel.

2 In a shallow dish, combine the flour with the salt and pepper. In a second shallow dish, whisk together the eggs and milk. In a third shallow dish, mix the breadcrumbs with the Italian seasoning, garlic powder, lemon zest, and Parmesan.

3 Season the chicken breasts with salt and pepper. Dip each chicken breast first into the flour mixture, then into the egg mixture, then coat with the breadcrumb mixture. Use one hand for the dry coatings and the other for the wet coatings to keep the process neat.

4 In a large skillet, heat the olive oil over medium heat until it is shimmering. Fry the chicken in batches until golden brown, 3 to 4 minutes per side or until they reach an internal temperature of 165°F on an instant-read thermometer. Drain on a paper towel–lined plate. Sprinkle with chopped parsley and serve with a lemon wedge.

Chicken Parmesan

Breaded cutlets from Chicken Milanese

2 cups marinara sauce

1½ cups shredded mozzarella

½ cup grated Parmesan

Fresh basil leaves, for garnish

1 Preheat your oven to 400°F. Spread a thin layer of marinara sauce in a 13-by-9-inch baking dish.

2 Place the fried chicken cutlets in the dish. Top each cutlet evenly with the marinara sauce, then sprinkle with the mozzarella and Parmesan. Bake for 20 to 25 minutes, until the cheese is bubbly and golden. Let cool and rest for 5 minutes before serving. Serve hot, garnished with fresh basil leaves.

HONEY SRIRACHA GRILLED CHICKEN *with* SPICY FRIED RICE

Craving something new for dinner? This dish gives you just the right kick of spice balanced with a touch of sweetness. And because I grew up in Indonesia, I thought we should pair it with a flavorful fried rice. Rice that's been refrigerated overnight is optimal for frying because it's drier. If you have only fresh rice, try to cool it in the fridge for a few hours before frying. Adding carrots, bell peppers, or corn to the fried rice can add color and nutritional value. —A

For the chicken

4 boneless, skinless chicken breasts (about 1½ pounds)

1 teaspoon salt

1 teaspoon freshly ground black pepper

⅓ cup honey

⅓ cup extra-virgin olive oil

2 tablespoons sriracha

For the fried rice

4 tablespoons butter, divided

1 egg, beaten

1 garlic clove, minced

1 teaspoon minced ginger

2 green onions, thinly sliced (white and green parts separated)

3 cups leftover cooked white rice, chilled

½ cup frozen peas

2 tablespoons sriracha

½ teaspoon salt

½ teaspoon ground white or black pepper

2 tablespoons soy sauce

1 teaspoon sesame oil

Sliced green onions and sesame seeds, for topping

1 Make the chicken: Place the chicken breasts between two pieces of parchment paper or plastic wrap and gently pound them using a meat mallet or rolling pin to an even thickness of about ¼ inch. Season each breast with the salt and pepper on both sides. Place the chicken in a gallon-size zip-top bag.

2 In a small bowl, mix together the honey, olive oil, and sriracha. Add about ¾ of the mixture to the bag with the chicken, reserving ¼ cup of the marinade for later. Massage the chicken in the bag until it's completely coated with the marinade. Refrigerate for a minimum of 1 hour.

3 Preheat your grill to medium high, about 450°F.

4 Grill the chicken breasts for 5 to 6 minutes on each side. Brush the chicken with the reserved marinade when flipping. Cook until the internal temperature reaches 165°F on an instant-read thermometer. Allow the chicken to rest for 5 minutes, then slice into strips. Set aside.

FAMILY
TRIP *to*
Indonesia

5 Make the fried rice: In a wok or large skillet, melt 1 tablespoon of butter over medium heat. Add the egg and scramble until cooked to your liking, then remove and set aside on a plate.

6 Melt the remaining 3 tablespoons of butter in the pan. Sauté the garlic, ginger, and the white parts of the green onions until fragrant, about 1 minute. Stir in the rice, peas, sriracha, salt, and pepper, mixing well. Fry for 3 to 4 minutes, until the rice turns golden brown. Lower heat and mix in the scrambled egg, soy sauce, and sesame oil.

7 Divide the rice among bowls and top with the chicken. Drizzle with any remaining marinade and top with the green parts of the green onions and sesame seeds.

One-Pot
JAMBALAYA
with CHICKEN

Looking for a healthier twist on a Louisiana classic? You have to try this
One-Pot Jambalaya with Chicken! Packed with brown rice, sausage, chicken, and a ton
of veggies, it has the perfect kick of Creole spice. My Louisiana family loves it,
and I get to sneak in one of my all-time favorite veggies: okra! You can substitute
another vegetable, such as zucchini or bell peppers, but you might be surprised
by how much you love okra once you try it. —A

3 tablespoons extra-virgin olive oil, divided

1 pound andouille chicken sausage or turkey kielbasa, sliced

1 medium yellow onion, chopped

3 stalks celery, chopped

1 green bell pepper, diced

2 garlic cloves, minced

2 tablespoons Creole seasoning (such as Tony Chachere's)

1 (14-ounce) can diced fire-roasted tomatoes

4 cups chicken broth

1¼ cups short-grain brown rice

1 (12-ounce) package of sliced frozen okra

1 cup shredded rotisserie chicken (about half of the chicken)

Sliced green onions and hot sauce, for topping

1 In a Dutch oven or a large heavy-bottomed pot with a lid, heat 2 tablespoons of olive oil over medium-high heat until shimmering. Add the sausage and cook, stirring, until lightly browned, 5 to 6 minutes. Remove the sausage from the pot and set aside on a plate.

2 Reduce heat to medium and add the remaining olive oil, along with the onion, celery, and bell pepper. Sauté until softened, 4 to 5 minutes. Add the garlic and Creole seasoning and sauté for about 1 minute, until the garlic is fragrant. Stir in the tomatoes, broth, and rice and bring the mixture to a boil. Cover, lower heat to medium low, and allow the mixture to simmer for 45 minutes, stirring every 10 minutes or so to prevent the rice from sticking to the pan.

3 Stir in the okra, chicken, and sausage. Cover and simmer on low for 10 to 15 minutes, stirring occasionally, until the liquid is fully absorbed and the rice is tender. Remove the pan from heat and fluff up the rice. Serve hot with green onions and hot sauce.

HOMESTYLE POT ROAST *with* GRAVY

There are some dishes that take you right back to your childhood, and for me, one of them is the Sunday pot roast. My mom would throw all the ingredients into a big pot and start it early in the morning; by the time we got back from church, it had simmered for hours and was ready to eat. Tender, full of flavor, and flat-out delicious, it's a dish she makes to this day, and it is the best! It's customizable to your family's taste; try roasting root vegetables such as turnips, parsnips, or sweet potatoes alongside the meat. —**A**

For the pot roast

1 tablespoon salt

1 tablespoon freshly ground black pepper

3 to 4 pounds boneless chuck roast

2 tablespoons extra-virgin olive oil

1 medium yellow onion, chopped

3 garlic cloves, minced

1 cup dry red wine

4 cups beef broth

¼ cup Worcestershire sauce

2 sprigs fresh thyme

2 sprigs fresh rosemary

1 bay leaf

1 pound baby carrots

1½ pounds Yukon Gold potatoes, quartered

For the gravy

6 tablespoons unsalted butter

½ cup all-purpose flour

3 cups beef broth, reserved from the pot

¾ teaspoon salt

½ teaspoon freshly ground black pepper

1 **Make the pot roast:** Preheat your oven to 275°F.

2 In a small bowl, mix the salt and pepper. Use about half of this mixture to season the roast on all sides.

3 In a Dutch oven, heat the olive oil over medium-high heat until shimmering. Add the roast to the pot and sear it on each side until nicely browned, 4 to 5 minutes per side. Remove from the pot and set aside on a plate.

4 Reduce heat to medium. Add the onion and sauté until soft, 4 to 5 minutes. Add the garlic and sauté until fragrant, about 1 minute. Pour in the red wine, scraping the bottom of the pot to loosen all the flavorful browned bits. Pour in the beef broth and bring the mixture to a simmer. Return the beef to the pot. Drizzle Worcestershire sauce over the roast and add the thyme, rosemary, and bay leaf. Cover the pot and place in the oven on the middle rack for 2 hours.

Recipe Continues

5 Remove the roast from the oven and add the carrots and potatoes. Season with the remaining salt and pepper. Return the pot to the oven and cook, covered, for another 2 hours, until the vegetables are tender and the roast pulls apart easily. Remove the roast to a cutting board and let stand for at least 10 minutes before serving. Discard the thyme, rosemary, and bay leaf. If you are making gravy, remove 3 cups of the beef broth from the pot. If the liquid has reduced too much during cooking, add enough water to bring the total to 3 cups.

6 **Make the gravy:** In a medium saucepan, melt the butter over medium heat. Add the flour and whisk until it looks thick and pasty. Whisk in the reserved cooking liquid from the pot and continue whisking until it thickens, 2 to 3 minutes. Season with the salt and pepper.

7 Slice the meat into bite-size pieces or gently shred with two forks. Serve with the warm gravy and vegetables.

Make This!

Check the roast for doneness toward the end of cooking. If the meat is not as tender as you'd like, you can cook it a bit longer. The total cooking time may vary depending on the size and cut of the roast.

❝ TENDER, *full of* **FLAVOR,** *and* **flat-out DELICIOUS**

GREEN CHILE CHICKEN ENCHILADAS

When it comes to a tasty, convenient family meal, Green Chile Chicken Enchiladas are at the top of our list. They're easy to make and perfect for those busy nights when you need a quick dinner. You can use store-bought canned sauce to make this recipe a breeze. If you're looking to substitute for the rotisserie chicken, cooked and shredded pork or beef is an excellent alternative. For a vegetarian option, consider using black beans or a mix of beans and quinoa for a protein-packed filling.

1 rotisserie chicken, shredded (about 2½ cups)

2 (10-ounce) cans green chile enchilada sauce, divided

2 cups shredded Monterey Jack cheese, divided

1 cup sour cream

10 medium corn tortillas

Chopped fresh cilantro, sliced green onions, and pico de gallo, for topping

1 Preheat your oven to 425°F. Grease a 13-by-9-inch baking dish.

2 In a large bowl, mix the chicken, one-third of the enchilada sauce, half the cheese, and the sour cream until combined. Spread a third of the sauce on the bottom of the prepared baking dish.

3 Soften the tortillas in a microwave between two damp paper towels for 30 seconds. Spoon the chicken mixture onto each tortilla, roll tightly, and place seam side down in the dish. Top with the remaining sauce and cheese.

4 Bake for 20 to 25 minutes, until the cheese is melted and golden. Serve hot, topped with chopped fresh cilantro, sliced green onions, and pico de gallo.

" A TASTY, convenient FAMILY MEAL

Make this!

While corn tortillas are traditional and provide a distinct taste and gluten-free option, flour tortillas can be used for a softer texture.

ONE-POT SOY GARLIC PASTA

Okay, here's the deal, I love garlic (I want it in every dish), and I also love a little spice. If are like me, this One-Pot Soy Garlic Pasta is going to rock your world. And get this: You can eat it hot or cold! Come on! I love taking this to potlucks; it's always the first to go. There's tender linguine tossed with ribbons of carrots and zucchini, all dressed up in a spicy, savory sauce and topped with juicy rotisserie chicken and crunchy peanuts. Yummmm! —A

For the sauce

¾ cup soy sauce

2 tablespoons brown sugar

2 tablespoons sriracha

2 teaspoons minced ginger

¼ cup fresh lime juice

½ teaspoon ground white pepper

For the pasta

1 pound linguine or spaghetti

3 tablespoons extra-virgin olive oil, divided

1 medium shallot, chopped

3 garlic cloves, minced

4 carrots, peeled into ribbons

3 zucchini, peeled into ribbons

1 rotisserie chicken, shredded (about 2½ cups)

2 cups bean sprouts

Thinly sliced green onions and crushed dry-roasted peanuts, for topping

1 **Make the sauce:** In a small bowl, whisk together the soy sauce, brown sugar, sriracha, ginger, lime juice, and pepper. Set aside.

2 **Make the pasta:** Cook the pasta in a large pot of boiling salted water until al dente. Drain, toss with 1 tablespoon of olive oil, and set aside.

3 In a wok or large skillet, heat the remaining olive oil over medium-high heat until hot. Add the shallot and sauté until translucent and slightly golden, 3 to 4 minutes. Add the garlic and sauté for another minute until fragrant. Add the carrots and zucchini and sauté for 2 to 3 minutes, until just tender yet still brightly colored. Reduce heat to medium low and add the cooked pasta, chicken, and reserved soy garlic sauce. Toss to combine and to coat the pasta with the sauce. Fold in the bean sprouts. Serve topped with thinly sliced green onions and crushed dry-roasted peanuts.

Skillet CHICKEN POT PIE

Do you remember those frozen Hungry Man pot pies? When my mom had to work nights, my sisters and I had to make dinner for ourselves and those were my go-to. I still crave them, so I was determined to recreate a version from scratch. This Skillet Chicken Pot Pie has everything: a flaky crust, creamy chicken filling, and all your favorite veggies. You can easily adapt this recipe to different baking dishes or ramekins by preparing the filling as directed, then distributing it into your chosen dishes and adjusting the cooking time accordingly (smaller portions will cook faster). —**J**

3 tablespoons extra-virgin olive oil

1 medium yellow onion, diced

4 carrots, peeled and diced

4 celery ribs, diced

2 garlic cloves, minced

¼ cup all-purpose flour

1 teaspoon dried sage

1 teaspoon dried marjoram

½ teaspoon dried rosemary

1 teaspoon salt

1 teaspoon freshly ground black pepper

¼ cup white wine

1 (10.5-ounce) can cream of chicken soup

2 cups chicken broth

1 rotisserie chicken, shredded (about 2½ cups)

½ cup frozen peas

½ cup frozen corn

1 (14.1-ounce) package refrigerated pie crusts (2 crusts)

Egg wash (1 large egg plus 1 tablespoon water or milk)

1 Preheat your oven to 375°F. Make a pie shield out of aluminum foil.

2 In a 12-inch cast-iron skillet, heat the olive oil over medium-high heat until shimmering. Add the onion, carrots, and celery and cook, stirring, for 5 to 6 minutes, until they soften. Add the garlic and sauté for about 1 minute, until fragrant. Stir in the flour, sage, marjoram, rosemary, salt, and pepper. Cook, stirring, until no floury bits remain.

3 Slowly add the wine to the skillet and cook for 1 to 2 minutes, scraping up any browned bits from the bottom of the skillet. Stir in the cream of chicken soup and the chicken broth until blended. Bring to a boil, then reduce heat and simmer for 4 to 5 minutes to thicken. Fold in the chicken, peas, and corn and cook for 3 to 4 minutes, until warmed through. Remove from heat.

4 On a floured surface, place one pie crust atop the other. Roll both crusts together into a single 14-inch-diameter circle. This thicker crust will help hold all the ingredients of the pot pie.

5 Drape the crust over the skillet, carefully tucking in the edges to seal the pie. Crimp the edges and cut slits in the top to allow steam to escape. Brush the crust with the egg wash and bake for 20 minutes with a baking sheet below to catch drips. Add the pie shield, then bake until the crust is golden brown, 15 to 20 minutes, for about 40 minutes total. Let stand for about 10 minutes before serving.

LASAGNA ROLL-UPS

Let us introduce you to the amazingness of lasagna roll-ups. Combine all the elements of a classic lasagna—creamy ricotta cheese, gooey mozzarella, and savory meat sauce—into a perfectly portioned, rolled-up serving topped with crisp melted cheese. It's a fun twist on traditional lasagna. Plus, making these roll-ups can be a fun family activity.

1 (15-ounce) container ricotta

1 large egg, beaten

1 cup grated Parmesan

¼ cup chopped fresh parsley

3 cups shredded mozzarella, divided

1 teaspoon salt

½ teaspoon freshly ground black pepper

2 tablespoons extra-virgin olive oil

½ medium yellow onion, diced

1 pound ground turkey

2 garlic cloves, minced

3 cups marinara sauce, divided

2 tablespoons Italian seasoning

1 pound lasagna sheets

Chopped fresh parsley, for topping

1 In a large bowl, mix together the ricotta, egg, Parmesan, parsley, 2½ cups of mozzarella, the salt, and pepper. Set aside.

2 In a large skillet, heat the olive oil over medium-high heat until shimmering. Add the onion and turkey and cook for 5 to 6 minutes, until the onion is soft and the turkey is browned, breaking up the turkey with the back of your spoon. Add the garlic and sauté for another minute until fragrant. Reduce heat to medium, stir in 1 cup of marinara sauce and the Italian seasoning, and simmer for 2 minutes. Set aside.

3 Lightly grease a 10-inch cast-iron skillet or a 9-inch-square baking dish with nonstick spray or cooking spray. Line 2 sheet pans with parchment paper.

4 Bring a large pot of salted water to a boil and cook the lasagna per package instructions, until al dente. Drain and rinse the lasagna and lay it out on the parchment paper so the sheets don't touch.

5 Spread 1 cup of marinara sauce evenly around the bottom of the skillet. Spread 2 tablespoons of the ricotta mixture evenly over each lasagna sheet, then spread a thin layer of the meat filling on top of the cheese. Roll the sheet up tightly so the meat and cheese are on the inside. Arrange vertically in the prepared cast-iron skillet, packing snugly to prevent any escapees. Drizzle the top with the remaining cup of marinara sauce and sprinkle with the remaining mozzarella. Bake for 22 to 25 minutes, until the edges are a bit crispy and the cheese is melty. Serve warm, sprinkled with chopped parsley.

Make this!

This recipe is easily scalable. If you are feeding a larger crowd, you can increase the quantities by 50 percent and assemble in a 12-inch cast-iron skillet.

Lemon Garlic
GRILLED CHICKEN

This recipe is a breeze to whip up; just a quick 30-minute marinade infuses the chicken with a tasty lemon garlic flavor that pairs well with any side dish you're craving, whether it's veggies, pasta, or a salad.

4 boneless, skinless chicken breasts (about 1½ pounds)

¾ cup lemon juice

⅓ cup extra-virgin olive oil

1 tablespoon minced garlic

2 teaspoons dried oregano

1 teaspoon salt

1 teaspoon freshly ground black pepper

1 Place the chicken breasts between two pieces of parchment paper or plastic wrap and gently pound them with a meat mallet or rolling pin to an even thickness of about ½ inch.

2 In a medium bowl, mix the lemon juice, olive oil, garlic, oregano, salt, and pepper. Reserve a ¼-cup portion of the marinade to brush onto the chicken while grilling. Then add the chicken and the remaining marinade to a large zip-top bag. Massage the chicken in the bag to ensure that it's fully coated. Marinate for 45 minutes on the counter or up to 3 hours in the refrigerator.

3 Preheat your outdoor grill to medium high.

4 Grill the chicken breasts for 5 minutes on one side. Flip them, apply the reserved marinade, and cook for 5 to 6 minutes or until the chicken reaches an internal temperature of 165°F. Allow to rest for 5 minutes before serving.

JACK working
the GRILL

ONE-POT SPINACH *and* PROSCIUTTO PASTA

This one-pot recipe is all about simplicity and flavor. You just
toss everything into a pot, and it transforms into something amazing.
It's so easy that it feels like an instant dinner.

2 tablespoons extra-virgin olive oil, divided, plus extra for drizzling

8 ounces sliced prosciutto, torn

1 pound linguine

1 pint cherry or grape tomatoes, quartered

1 medium yellow onion, thinly sliced

4 garlic cloves, minced

2 teaspoons minced ginger

½ teaspoon red pepper flakes

2 teaspoons salt

1 teaspoon freshly ground black pepper

4 cups chicken broth

2 cups packed baby spinach

¼ cup freshly grated Parmesan, plus more for topping

Fresh basil leaves, for topping

1 In a Dutch oven or large, heavy-bottomed pot with a lid, heat 1 tablespoon of olive oil over medium-high heat until shimmering. Add the prosciutto and sauté for 3 to 4 minutes, until nice and crisp. Remove from the pot and set aside.

2 To the same pot, add the remaining tablespoon of olive oil along with the linguine, tomatoes, onion, garlic, ginger, red pepper flakes, salt, and pepper. Pour in the chicken broth and bring the mixture to a boil over medium-high heat. Cook the pasta at a gentle boil for about 8 minutes, stirring occasionally, until most of the liquid has evaporated.

3 Reduce the heat to medium, add the spinach, and stir until it begins to wilt and the liquid is saucy, about 8 minutes. Fold in the prosciutto and stir in the grated Parmesan. Serve hot, topped with grated Parmesan and a few fresh basil leaves.

Marinated SKIRT STEAK *with* CHIMICHURRI

We have a few friends who are "foodies," and when they come over for dinner, this is the dish we make to impress them. The zesty, herb-packed chimichurri adds a burst of freshness. Serve it on the side, and watch everyone fight over it! You'll want to soak the steak in the marinade for a few hours for maximum flavor.

For the steak

¼ cup extra-virgin olive oil

¼ cup dry red wine

¼ cup soy sauce

2 tablespoons honey

2 teaspoons minced garlic

½ teaspoon red pepper flakes

1½ pounds skirt steak

1 teaspoon salt

2 teaspoons freshly ground black pepper

For the chimichurri

⅛ cup diced red onion

1 garlic clove, minced

1 tablespoon red wine vinegar

2 tablespoons lemon juice

½ teaspoon salt

⅓ cup fresh parsley leaves and tender stems, packed

¼ cup fresh cilantro leaves and tender stems, packed

1 teaspoon dried oregano

¼ cup extra-virgin olive oil

1 **Marinate the steak:** In a medium bowl, whisk together the olive oil, wine, soy sauce, honey, garlic, and red pepper flakes. Pour into a gallon-size zip-top bag.

2 Season the steak with the salt and pepper and add to the marinade. Seal the bag and give the steak a little massage to make sure it's fully coated with the marinade. Marinate in the refrigerator for at least 2 hours.

3 **Make the chimichurri:** In a food processor, pulse the onion, garlic, red wine vinegar, lemon juice, and salt until roughly blended. Add the parsley, cilantro, oregano, and olive oil, and pulse again until the mixture is just blended but still has texture. Transfer the chimichurri to a bowl and refrigerate until serving.

4 **Grill the steak:** Remove the steak from the refrigerator 30 minutes before grilling to reach room temperature.

5 Preheat your grill to high heat.

6 Remove the steak from the marinade. For medium rare, grill uncovered for about 4 minutes per side or until the internal temperature reaches 130°F on an instant-read thermometer. If you prefer your steak more done, cook for 5 to 6 minutes per side for medium to medium well. Allow it to rest for 5 minutes before slicing against the grain. Serve topped with the chimichurri.

One-Pot ORECCHIETTE with CHICKEN SAUSAGE, FENNEL, and ASPARAGUS

Ange and I try to go away for the weekend every November to celebrate our anniversary with a road trip up the coast (big thank-you to my mom for watching the kids for us over the years so we could get away). On one of those trips, we stumbled across an Italian restaurant deep in the redwoods. The waitress recommended an orecchiette dish that we both loved. I knew I had to recreate it at home, and it has quickly become one of our favorite family meals. With ingredients such as fennel, lemon juice, white wine, and capers, you'll feel as though you are in a fancy restaurant right in your own home! —**J**

3 tablespoons extra-virgin olive oil

1 pound uncooked Italian chicken sausage, casing removed

1 large fennel bulb, finely chopped

3 garlic cloves, minced

1 teaspoon salt

½ teaspoon freshly ground black pepper

¼ teaspoon crushed red pepper flakes

1 cup dry white wine

2 cups chicken broth

½ cup lemon juice

2 tablespoons capers

8 ounces orecchiette

½ pound asparagus spears, cut into 2-inch pieces

½ cup shaved Pecorino Romano, for topping

1 In a large, high-sided skillet or Dutch oven, heat the olive oil over medium heat until shimmering. Add the sausage and fennel to the pan, and cook, stirring and breaking up the sausage, until browned, about 5 minutes. Stir in the garlic, salt, black pepper, and red pepper flakes and cook over medium heat until the garlic is fragrant, about 1 minute.

2 Pour in the white wine, allowing it to come to a boil, and scrape up any brown bits from the bottom of the pot. Reduce heat and simmer for about 3 minutes to reduce slightly. Add the chicken broth and increase the heat to medium-high, to bring it to a boil. Once boiling, reduce heat to medium and add the lemon juice and capers. Stir in the orecchiette and asparagus and continue to cook over medium heat for 12 to 14 minutes, stirring occasionally, until the pasta is al dente and the asparagus is tender.

3 Serve hot, topped with shaved Pecorino Romano.

Pan-Seared SALMON *with* SUNFLOWER GREMOLATA

This recipe sounds fancy, but it's actually really simple and tastes amazing. The secret ingredient is the sunflower seeds! They add a unique flavor and crunch that set this dish apart.

For the gremolata

1 cup finely minced fresh parsley

½ cup unsalted sunflower seeds, roasted and chopped

¼ cup fresh lemon juice

2 tablespoons lemon zest

2 garlic cloves, minced

2 teaspoons salt

2 teaspoons freshly ground black pepper

For the salmon

4 (8-ounce) salmon fillets, skin on

1 teaspoon salt

1 teaspoon freshly ground black pepper

1 tablespoon unsalted butter

1 tablespoon canola oil

Lemon wedges, for serving

1 **Make the gremolata:** In a medium bowl, combine the parsley, sunflower seeds, lemon juice, lemon zest, garlic, salt, and pepper. Set aside.

2 **Make the salmon:** Pat the salmon dry with paper towels and season both sides with the salt and pepper.

3 In a 12-inch cast-iron or heavy stainless-steel skillet, heat the butter and oil over medium-high heat until the butter is foamy and begins to brown. It is crucial that the pan be very hot before you add the salmon to ensure proper crisping. Carefully place the fillets in the skillet skin side up. Cook undisturbed for 5 to 6 minutes, until the flesh appears opaque about three quarters of the way up the fillet. Flip the salmon using a spatula. Reduce heat to medium and cook skin side down for an additional 2 to 4 minutes or until the internal temperature is 130°F on an instant-read thermometer. Serve warm or at room temperature with lemon wedges, topped with the gremolata.

Sheet Pan CHICKEN *and* STEAK FAJITAS

Sheet pan dinners are the best! Most of the prep is done ahead of time, and, as with one-pot meals, there isn't a ton of cleanup—perfect for those busy weekday evenings! Our kids love sheet pan fajitas. What's great about them is that you can make any combination of ingredients that you want: chicken, steak, or veggies. We have meat eaters and vegetarians in our extended family, so this is a great dish when you need to have multiple options. Josh adds his homemade southwestern seasoning, but a ready-to-go fajita spice packet will work just as well. —A

2 small boneless, skinless chicken breasts (about 12 ounces)

12 ounces strip steak

¼ cup soy sauce

¼ cup lime juice

1 garlic clove, minced

1 (1-ounce) packet taco seasoning, divided

1 red bell pepper, cut into strips

1 green bell pepper, cut into strips

1 medium white onion, sliced

2 tablespoons extra-virgin olive oil

1 lime

3 tablespoons roughly chopped cilantro, for topping

8 flour or corn tortillas, warmed

Shredded cheddar cheese, sour cream, pico de gallo, and guacamole, for topping

1 Preheat your oven to 400°F. Line a large sheet pan with parchment paper.

2 Cut the chicken and steak into 1-inch strips against the grain. In a large zip-top bag, combine the chicken and steak with the soy sauce, lime juice, garlic, and half of the taco seasoning. Seal the bag and massage to ensure that the meat is well coated with the marinade. Place in the refrigerator and marinate for at least 1 hour.

3 Place the red bell pepper, green bell pepper, and onion in a medium bowl. Toss with the olive oil and the remaining taco seasoning until well coated. Spread the veggies on the prepared sheet pan and roast for 10 minutes. Remove from the oven and, using tongs, add the steak and chicken to the sheet pan in an even layer. Discard the marinade liquid. Bake for 10 minutes more.

4 Switch the oven to broil. Broil the meat and veggies for 3 to 5 minutes, until the vegetables are slightly charred and the chicken reaches an internal temperature of 165°F on an instant-read thermometer. Remove from the oven, drizzle with lime juice, and sprinkle with chopped cilantro. Serve with warm tortillas and your favorite fajita toppings.

Make this!

To make your own taco seasoning, combine 2½ teaspoons chili powder, 1½ teaspoons cumin, ½ teaspoon paprika, ½ teaspoon oregano, 1 teaspoon freshly ground black pepper, and 1 teaspoon salt.

PROSCIUTTO-STUFFED CHICKEN

This prosciutto-stuffed chicken, with its light lemony sauce, creamy Boursin, sun-dried tomatoes, fresh basil, and savory prosciutto, is a standout. It's simple enough for a weeknight but special enough to serve to guests—bright, rich, and full of flavor.

4 thinly sliced boneless, skinless chicken breasts (about 1¼ pounds)

1 teaspoon salt

1 teaspoon freshly ground black pepper

1 teaspoon paprika

1 (5.3-ounce) block herb and garlic Boursin

4 ounces prosciutto (6 to 8 slices)

¼ cup sun-dried tomatoes packed in oil, drained and chopped

8 fresh basil leaves, torn, plus extra for garnish

2 tablespoons extra-virgin olive oil

½ cup chicken broth

¼ cup freshly squeezed lemon juice

1 Preheat your oven to 450°F. Lightly grease an 8-by-8-inch baking dish.

2 Place the chicken breasts between two pieces of parchment paper or plastic wrap and gently pound them to an even thickness of about ¼ inch with a meat mallet or rolling pin. Pat dry and season each side with the salt, pepper, and paprika.

3 Spread a generous layer of Boursin over the chicken breasts, then top with a layer of prosciutto, tomatoes, and a few basil leaves. Carefully roll up each breast, starting from the broad side. Secure the rolls with toothpicks.

4 In a medium skillet, heat the olive oil over medium-high heat until shimmering. Brown the chicken rolls for 2 to 3 minutes on each side. Transfer the rolls to the prepared baking dish. Add the broth and lemon juice. Bake for 10 minutes, then turn over and baste with the broth mixture. Return to the oven and bake for 5 to 7 minutes or until the internal temperature reaches 165°F on an instant-read thermometer. Let rest for 5 minutes, remove the toothpicks, and slice. Serve hot with some of the cooking liquid ladled over, garnished with torn fresh basil leaves.

Sheet Pan GNOCCHI *with* SAUSAGE *and* TOMATOES

There is one sheet pan dish that Ange asks me to make over and over.
It's Gnocchi with Sausage and Tomatoes: gnocchi, succulent tomatoes, and a zesty
sauce made with tangy lemon, garlic (her favorite), and savory capers on a single sheet
pan. It's light and refreshing and won't leave you feeling too heavy, making it the
perfect choice for a summer meal. This one gets a big Ange thumbs-up. —**J**

1 pound Italian sausage, casings removed

1 (12-ounce) package gnocchi, refrigerated or shelf stable

1 pint cherry tomatoes

½ pound broccolini, trimmed and cut into 2-inch pieces

1 yellow squash, cut into 1-inch pieces

3 tablespoons extra-virgin olive oil

3 garlic cloves, minced

¼ cup capers, drained

1 teaspoon salt

1 teaspoon pepper

2 tablespoons unsalted butter, melted

¼ cup lemon juice

Shaved Pecorino Romano and chopped fresh basil, for topping

1 Preheat your oven to 425°F. Line a large sheet pan with parchment paper.

2 Break the sausages into medium-size chunks. Arrange evenly on the prepared sheet pan.

3 In a large bowl, combine the gnocchi, tomatoes, broccolini, squash, olive oil, garlic, and capers and toss until everything is evenly coated. Season with the salt and pepper. Spread the gnocchi mixture onto the sheet pan, nestling it around the sausage pieces.

4 Bake for 50 to 60 minutes, rotating the baking sheet and stirring the mixture halfway through to ensure even cooking. Transfer the mixture to a large serving bowl and toss with the melted butter and lemon juice. Serve warm, topped with shaved Pecorino Romano and chopped fresh basil.

Skillet COTTAGE PIE

My sophomore year in college, I did a semester abroad in London. I loved it! I studied William Shakespeare, Thomas Hardy, and William Wordsworth. It was chilly and rained a lot, and I grew to be very fond of cottage pie. It's one of those hearty dishes that is perfect for a chilly night. We make ours in a skillet and serve it nice and hot. Consider adding a pinch of nutmeg to the mashed potatoes for extra depth of flavor. For a smokier flavor, add a dash of smoked paprika to the meat mixture. If you're looking for a traditional shepherd's pie, use ground lamb instead of beef. —**A**

For the mashed potatoes

2 pounds russet potatoes, peeled and cut into 1-inch pieces

½ cup butter, cut into chunks

⅓ cup sour cream

½ teaspoon garlic powder

½ teaspoon salt

¼ teaspoon ground freshly ground black pepper

½ cup grated cheddar cheese

For the meat filling

2 tablespoons extra-virgin olive oil

1 medium yellow onion, diced

3 carrots, peeled and diced

3 celery ribs, diced

1 pound 90% lean ground beef

2 garlic cloves, minced

1 teaspoon dried parsley

1 teaspoon dried rosemary

1 teaspoon dried thyme

1 teaspoon salt

1 teaspoon freshly ground black pepper

2 tablespoons all-purpose flour

2 tablespoons tomato paste

½ cup red wine

½ cup beef broth

2 tablespoons Worcestershire sauce

½ cup frozen peas

½ cup frozen corn kernels

For the topping

1 tablespoon unsalted butter

½ cup plain breadcrumbs

1 teaspoon fresh minced rosemary

½ teaspoon salt

½ teaspoon freshly ground black pepper

1 **Make the mashed potatoes:** Add the potatoes to a large pot with salted water and bring to a boil. Cook for 10 to 15 minutes, until soft and easily pierced with a fork. Drain and return them to the pot. Add the butter, sour cream, garlic powder, salt, and pepper. Mash until smooth and everything is melted and combined. Stir in the cheddar cheese and cover the pot. Set aside.

2 **Make the meat filling:** Preheat your oven to 400°F.

3 In a 12-inch cast-iron skillet, heat the olive oil over medium heat until shimmering. Add the onion, carrots, and celery to the skillet and sauté for 5 to 6 minutes, until soft. Add the beef and cook, breaking up with the back of a wooden spoon, until browned, about 8 minutes. Add the garlic and cook until fragrant, about 1 minute. Sprinkle in the parsley, rosemary, and thyme and season with the salt and pepper. Add the flour and tomato paste. Stir until well incorporated and no clumps of tomato paste remain. Add the red wine and let the wine reduce for 1 to 2 minutes, scraping up the browned bits. Add the beef broth, Worcestershire sauce, peas, and corn. Stir together and cook for another 1 to 2 minutes. Set aside.

4 **Make the topping:** In a small saucepan, melt the butter over medium heat. Add the breadcrumbs, rosemary, salt, and pepper. Cook, stirring, until the breadcrumbs start to brown, about 2 minutes. Remove from heat.

5 **Assemble the pie:** Spoon the mashed potatoes on top of the meat mixture and spread to the edges of the skillet. Use a fork to create lines on top of the mashed potatoes. Sprinkle the breadcrumb mixture evenly over the mashed potatoes.

6 Set the skillet on a large sheet pan to catch any drips and bake for 20 to 25 minutes, until the edges and ridges are golden brown and the breadcrumbs are browned and crisp. Remove from the oven and let cool for 5 minutes before serving.

Make this!

If you don't have a cast-iron skillet, you can prepare the meat mixture in a stovetop skillet, then transfer it into an 11-by-7-inch baking dish.

Spicy SOY GARLIC TURKEY BOWL

Ground turkey is a go-to in our kitchen, especially when we're cooking meals for the family, but this versatile recipe also works with ground beef or plant-based ground meat. Add fresh bok choy, chopped kimchi, and some pickled radishes for a tangy twist that perfectly complements the sweet and savory flavors. Last but not least, drizzle some spicy red curry mayo over it to tie the flavors together.

For the rice

1 cup jasmine rice

1½ cups water

½ teaspoon salt

For the radishes

1 tablespoon apple cider vinegar

1 tablespoon sesame oil

2 green onions, sliced

1 teaspoon salt

1 teaspoon freshly ground black pepper

3 ounces radishes (about 3 to 4), sliced into thin rounds

For the spicy sauce

¼ cup mayonnaise

2 tablespoons red curry paste

1 tablespoon honey

For the turkey

¼ cup soy sauce

¼ cup brown sugar

2 garlic cloves, minced

1 teaspoon minced ginger

¼ teaspoon red pepper flakes

1 tablespoon coconut oil

1½ pounds ground turkey

2 stalks baby bok choy, chopped

Sliced green onions and sesame seeds, for topping

1 **Make the rice:** Combine the rice, water, and salt in a saucepan and cook over medium high until boiling. Reduce the heat to medium low and cook for 10 to 15 minutes, until the water has been absorbed. Fluff with a fork, cover, and set aside.

2 **Make the radishes:** In a small bowl, whisk together the vinegar, sesame oil, green onions, salt, and pepper. Add the radishes and toss to coat. Cover and set aside.

3 **Make the spicy sauce:** In a second small bowl, mix the mayonnaise, red curry paste, and honey. Cover and refrigerate until the dish is ready to serve.

4 **Make the turkey:** In a third small bowl, mix the soy sauce, brown sugar, garlic, ginger, and red pepper flakes and set aside.

5 In a large skillet, heat the coconut oil over medium-high heat until shimmering. Add the turkey and cook for 5 to 6 minutes, breaking it into small pieces, until browned. Add the bok choy and cook, stirring occasionally, for 2 to 3 minutes, until it softens. Pour the reserved soy sauce mixture over the turkey mix and stir until everything is nicely coated. Divide the rice, turkey mixture, and radishes among bowls. Drizzle with the spicy sauce and top with sliced green onions and sesame seeds.

SWEET *and* SPICY CHICKEN

We love combining sweet and spicy flavors. This chicken is crisp and coated in a deliciously sticky, spicy sweet sauce. If you don't want to go out to dinner but want a meal that feels as though you did, this is the perfect entree. Serve over rice, noodles, or steamed veggies.

For the sauce

½ cup orange juice

¼ cup lemon juice

2 tablespoons rice vinegar

2 tablespoons soy sauce

2 tablespoons water

1½ tablespoons cornstarch

1 tablespoon sriracha

1 tablespoon brown sugar

2 teaspoons sesame oil

2 garlic cloves, minced

2 green onions, thinly sliced

½ teaspoon red pepper flakes

For the chicken

2 eggs

½ cup milk (2% or whole)

½ cup flour

¼ cup cornstarch

1¼ pounds boneless, skinless chicken breasts, cut into 1-inch pieces

2 teaspoons salt

2 teaspoons freshly ground black pepper

Canola oil, for frying

Cooked white rice, for serving

Sliced green onions, and sesame seeds, for topping

1 **Make the sauce:** In a small bowl, whisk together the orange juice, lemon juice, rice vinegar, soy sauce, water, cornstarch, sriracha, and brown sugar.

2 In a medium skillet, warm the sesame oil over medium heat. Add the garlic, green onions, and red pepper flakes and sauté for 1 to 2 minutes, until fragrant. Pour the orange juice mixture into the skillet and cook, stirring, for 2 to 3 minutes, until well combined and beginning to thicken. Remove from heat and set aside.

3 **Make the chicken:** In a large bowl, whisk together the eggs, milk, flour, and cornstarch until smooth. Season the chicken with the salt and pepper, then add it to the batter bowl. Use a large fork to stir the mixture, ensuring that the chicken pieces are coated with batter.

4 In a large, high-sided skillet or wok, heat 2 inches of oil over medium-high heat until the oil is shimmering or a pinch of flour sizzles when added. Add the chicken pieces in batches and fry for 6 to 8 minutes, until they're golden brown and the internal temperature reaches 165°F on an instant-read thermometer. With a slotted spoon, transfer to a paper towel–lined plate.

5 Discard almost all the surplus oil from the skillet. Pour the sauce into the pan and heat over medium heat until slightly thickened. Stir the crisp chicken into the sauce so each piece is coated. Serve over rice, sprinkled with sliced green onions and sesame seeds.

Mom's Homestyle CHICKEN and NOODLES with DUMPLINGS

This chicken and noodles recipe is my ultimate comfort food, complete with homemade dumplings. My mom still whips up her special version whenever I visit. I've loved it since I was a kid. Tender chicken, hearty noodles, and homemade dumplings mingle in a rich, savory broth. This isn't one of those fussy, complicated dishes; it's simple, heartfelt cooking at its best. **—J**

For the soup

2 tablespoons extra-virgin olive oil

1 medium onion, chopped

2 carrots, peeled and diced

2 celery ribs, diced

3 garlic cloves, minced

1 teaspoon dried thyme

1 teaspoon dried parsley

1 teaspoon salt

1 teaspoon freshly ground black pepper

8 cups chicken broth

1 (16-ounce) package frozen egg noodles

1 rotisserie chicken, shredded (about 2½ cups)

For the dumplings

2 cups all-purpose flour

1 tablespoon baking powder

½ teaspoon salt

1 cup milk (2% or whole)

1 tablespoon melted butter

1 Make the soup: In a Dutch oven or large soup pot, heat the olive oil over medium-high heat until shimmering. Add the onion, carrots, and celery and cook, stirring, until they start to soften, 5 to 7 minutes. Add the garlic and cook until fragrant, about 1 minute. Stir in the thyme, parsley, salt, and pepper. Pour in the chicken broth and bring to a boil over medium-high heat. Drop the frozen egg noodles into the broth and reduce heat to low. Simmer for about 10 minutes.

2 Make the dumplings: While the soup is simmering, in a medium bowl, combine the flour, baking powder, and salt. Stir in the milk and melted butter until combined and a sticky dough forms.

3 After the noodles have been cooking for 10 minutes, drop large spoonfuls of the dumpling dough into the pot, trying not to crowd the surface of the liquid. Cover the pot with a lid and allow the dumplings to steam for 15 to 20 minutes, until they are firm. Remove the dumplings from the pot and set aside on a plate.

4 Stir in the shredded chicken and continue to simmer for about 5 minutes, until the chicken is thoroughly heated. Divide the hot chicken and noodles into bowls and top each serving with a dumpling or two.

TURKEY BURRITO BOWL *over Mexican Rice*

This recipe is dedicated to my old roommate Devon. When we met in our early years in Los Angeles, we were living on a very fixed budget, and he came up with a low-cost turkey burrito bowl that quickly became a staple. What makes this burrito bowl great is its endless potential for customization—add diced bell peppers or jalapeños for a kick of heat, omit the beans if they're not your thing, or enjoy it over rice or lettuce. Despite the variations I've tried over the years, the simplicity and comfort of this bowl always draw me back. And honestly, I don't think that will ever change. —**J**

For the rice

2 tablespoons extra-virgin olive oil

½ medium white onion, diced

2 garlic cloves, minced

1½ cups long-grain white rice, rinsed

1 (10-ounce) can diced tomatoes and chiles

2 teaspoons cumin

½ teaspoon salt

2 cups chicken broth

2 tablespoons roughly chopped cilantro

Juice of 1 lime

For the turkey

1 tablespoon extra-virgin olive oil

1 pound ground turkey

3 green onions, chopped

½ green bell pepper, diced

½ red bell pepper, diced

1 (1-ounce) packet taco seasoning

1 teaspoon salt

½ teaspoon freshly ground black pepper

1 (14.5-ounce) can black beans, drained and rinsed

½ cup frozen corn

1 (4-ounce) can diced green chiles

¾ cup chicken broth or water

2 tablespoons roughly chopped cilantro

Shredded lettuce and shredded Mexican cheese blend, for serving

1 **Make the rice:** In a medium Dutch oven or deep skillet with a lid, heat the olive oil over medium heat until shimmering. Add the onion and sauté for 5 to 8 minutes, until soft. Add the garlic and sauté until fragrant, about 1 minute. Add the rice and cook for an additional 2 minutes until fragrant and lightly toasted. Stir in the tomatoes, cumin, salt, and chicken broth. Bring the mixture to a boil. Reduce heat and let simmer for about 15 minutes or until all the liquid has been absorbed. Remove from heat and fluff the rice with a fork. Stir in the cilantro and lime juice. Cover and set aside.

2 **Make the turkey:** In a large skillet, warm the olive oil over medium-high heat until shimmering. Add the ground turkey and cook, breaking it apart with a wooden spoon, for about 5 minutes, until lightly brown. Add the green onions, green bell pepper, and red bell pepper. Sauté for 4 to 5 minutes, until tender. Lower heat to medium and add the taco seasoning, salt, and pepper. Cook for 1 minute, then add the black beans, corn, green chiles, and chicken broth. Stir to combine and bring to a gentle boil. Simmer for about 10 minutes uncovered or until most of the liquid has evaporated, stirring occasionally. Remove from heat and fold in the cilantro. Divide the rice and turkey among bowls and top generously with shredded lettuce and shredded Mexican cheese blend.

Make this!

To make your own taco seasoning, combine
2½ teaspoons chili powder, 1½ teaspoons cumin,
½ teaspoon paprika, ½ teaspoon oregano, 1 teaspoon
freshly ground black pepper, and 1 teaspoon salt.

Southwest CHICKEN BURGERS *with* AVOCADO CORN SALSA

If you want to impress your neighbors at your next BBQ, this is the dish for you. The avocado corn salsa is the secret weapon. Diced avocados, zesty lime juice, fresh cilantro, and sweet corn come together to make the perfect topping for these juicy chicken burgers. Make sure to have some chips on hand, because this salsa is so good that you'll want to scoop up every last bite.

For the salsa

2 large ripe avocados, diced

1 cup frozen corn, thawed

2 tablespoons extra-virgin olive oil

¼ cup lime juice

1 teaspoon salt

½ teaspoon freshly ground black pepper

⅛ teaspoon cayenne

2 tablespoons chopped fresh cilantro

For the burgers

1½ pounds ground chicken

1 (4-ounce) can diced green chiles

¼ cup mayonnaise

1 cup shredded Mexican cheese blend

2 green onions, sliced

1 (1-ounce) packet taco seasoning

6 hamburger buns, toasted (optional)

1 **Make the salsa:** In a medium bowl, combine the avocados, corn, olive oil, lime juice, salt, black pepper, cayenne, and cilantro. Cover and set aside in the refrigerator.

2 **Make the burgers:** In a large bowl, mix the chicken, green chiles, mayonnaise, Mexican cheese blend, green onions, and taco seasoning until combined. Using a ½-cup scoop or your hands, create 6 firmly packed patties.

3 Preheat your outdoor grill to medium high and lightly oil the grill grates. Grill the chicken burgers for about 6 minutes on each side until the internal temperature reaches 165°F on an instant-read thermometer. Place the chicken burgers on the toasted buns, if desired, and serve topped with the avocado corn salsa. This is also delicious served bunless!

Make this!

To make your own taco/fajita seasoning, combine 2½ teaspoons chili powder, 1½ teaspoons cumin, ½ teaspoon paprika, ½ teaspoon oregano, 1 teaspoon freshly ground black pepper, and 1 teaspoon salt.

Cookies

Cowboy COOKIES

This one is for my family in Texas. My grandparents had big pecan trees in their front yard, and I have a vivid memory of sitting in their living room watching television—picture one of those televisions that sat inside a faux wood credenza and didn't have a remote control so you had to get up and turn the knob to change the channels—and shelling pecans. This recipe takes the classic chocolate chip cookie to a whole new level, giving you a cookie that's not too sweet but packed with all the good stuff. I'm pretty sure that Lena and Finis Kinsey would be proud that we included a few pecan recipes in this book! —**A**

2¼ cups all-purpose flour

1 teaspoon baking soda

1 teaspoon ground cinnamon

½ teaspoon salt

1 cup unsalted butter, softened

1 cup light brown sugar, packed

½ cup granulated sugar

2 large eggs, room temperature

2 teaspoons vanilla extract

2 cups old-fashioned rolled oats

¾ cup unsweetened flaked coconut

½ cup raw pecans, chopped

1 cup semisweet chocolate chips, plus more for topping

Flaky sea salt, for topping

1 In a medium bowl, whisk together the flour, baking soda, cinnamon, and salt. Set aside.

2 In the bowl of a stand mixer fitted with a paddle or a large bowl with a hand mixer, beat the butter until creamy. Add the brown sugar and granulated sugar and beat until light and fluffy, 2 to 3 minutes. Add the eggs one at a time, mixing after each addition, and then the vanilla extract, mixing for 1 to 2 minutes, until combined.

3 Gradually add the flour mixture and mix on low until just combined, scraping down the sides of the bowl as needed. The mixture will be wet and sticky. Turn the mixer to low and add the oats. Using a spatula, fold in the coconut, pecans, and chocolate chips. Cover the bowl with plastic wrap and chill in the fridge for at least 1 hour. This allows the oats time to absorb some of the moisture.

4 When you're ready to bake, preheat your oven to 350°F. Line two baking sheets with parchment paper.

5 Using a cookie scoop or spoon, scoop the dough into golf ball–size balls. Place them on the prepared baking sheets 2 inches apart.

6 Bake each batch, one baking sheet at a time, for 12 to 14 minutes, rotating the baking sheet halfway through baking until the edges are golden brown and look set. While the cookies are still warm, top with some extra chocolate chips and flaky sea salt for a delicious final touch. Cool on a wire rack.

Birthday Cake CRINKLE COOKIES

These cookies are among my top five cookies of all time, which is no easy feat. Not only do they taste amazing, but they also look so festive with their colorful sprinkles. After all, as Angela on *The Office* would agree, you can never have too many sprinkles! (Just don't let Dwight near them.) —**J**

2½ cups all-purpose flour

1½ teaspoons baking powder

½ teaspoon salt

½ cup unsalted butter, room temperature

1 cup granulated sugar

2 large eggs, room temperature

2 teaspoons vanilla extract

½ cup rainbow sprinkles

⅓ cup powdered sugar

1 In a medium bowl, whisk together the flour, baking powder, and salt. Set aside.

2 In the bowl of a stand mixer fitted with a paddle attachment or a large bowl with a hand mixer, beat the butter for about 1 minute, until creamy. Add the sugar and beat until light and fluffy, 2 to 3 minutes. Add the eggs, one at a time, mixing after each edition, and then the vanilla extract and mix until smooth. Add half the flour mixture and mix on low speed until just combined. Add the remaining flour mixture and beat until the dough just comes together. It will be thick and pull away from the sides of the bowl. Using a spatula, fold in the sprinkles. Cover the bowl with plastic wrap and refrigerate for 1 to 2 hours.

3 When you're ready to bake, preheat your oven to 350°F. Line two 18-by-13-inch baking sheets with parchment paper.

4 Add the powdered sugar to a plate. Using a cookie scoop or spoon, scoop the dough into golf ball–size balls. Roll the balls in the powdered sugar, coating them thoroughly. Place them on the prepared baking sheets about 2 inches apart.

5 Bake each batch, one baking sheet at a time, for 12 to 14 minutes, rotating the baking sheet halfway through, until the edges are set but the centers are still soft. Transfer each baking sheet from the oven to a wire rack and cool completely. Store the cookies in an airtight container for up to four days.

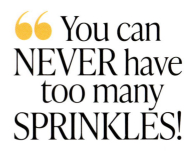

❝ You can NEVER have too many SPRINKLES!

PEPPERNUTS

Do you have a favorite childhood cookie that brings back holiday memories? For me, it's these amazing Peppernuts. I vividly remember sneaking a bowl of them off the holiday dessert table at a party and eating pretty much all of them. I couldn't resist their unique flavor, which reminded me of a combination of crunchy biscotti and gingerbread. So good. Don't be fooled by their size; these Peppernuts pack a punch of flavor thanks to cinnamon, cloves, nutmeg, white pepper, and a secret ingredient: anise! I make them every year around the holidays, Cade has also become obsessed with them. I bet after trying this recipe, you will be, too! —**J**

1¾ cups all-purpose flour, plus more for dusting

1 teaspoon ground cinnamon

½ teaspoon ground ginger

¼ teaspoon ground cloves

¼ teaspoon ground white pepper

½ teaspoon baking soda

½ teaspoon salt

½ cup unsalted butter, room temperature

¾ cup light brown sugar, packed

1 large egg, room temperature

1 teaspoon anise extract

1 In a medium bowl, whisk together the flour, cinnamon, ginger, cloves, pepper, baking soda, and salt. Set aside.

2 In the bowl of a stand mixer fitted with a paddle attachment or a large bowl with a hand mixer, beat the butter until creamy. Add the sugar and beat until light and fluffy, 2 to 3 minutes. Add the egg and then the anise extract, mixing for 1 to 2 minutes until combined. Gradually add half the flour mixture and mix on low until just combined, scraping down the sides of the bowl as needed. Add the remaining flour mixture and mix again until just combined.

3 Shape the dough into an 8-by-8-inch square and wrap tightly in plastic wrap. Chill the dough in the refrigerator for at least 30 minutes.

4 When you're ready to bake, preheat your oven to 350°F. Line two baking sheets with parchment paper.

5 Place the chilled dough on a lightly floured surface and, with a bench scraper or sharp knife, divide the dough into 8 equal pieces. Roll each piece into a long ½-inch-thick rope and lay the ropes next to each other on the floured surface. Chop into ½-inch bites using the same bench scraper or knife.

6 Place the dough bites on the prepared baking sheets with enough space between them not to touch. Gently press down on each piece with your thumb to flatten it out just a bit.

7 Bake each batch, one baking sheet at a time, for 12 to 14 minutes, rotating the baking sheet halfway through, until they turn golden brown. Let them cool on the baking sheet before storing them in an airtight container.

Brown Butter CHOCOLATE CHUNK COOKIES

If you're intimidated by the idea of making brown butter, don't be.
It might take a couple of tries to get it right, but once you know how, it's absolutely
worth it. These cookies are thinner and crisper than I usually make, but the
caramelized brown butter, dark brown sugar, and touch of sea salt create
a crisp, chewy texture that's irresistible. —**J**

2¼ cups all-purpose flour

1 teaspoon baking soda

½ teaspoon salt

1 cup unsalted butter

1½ cups dark brown sugar, packed

½ cup granulated sugar

2 large eggs, room temperature

1 tablespoon vanilla extract

1½ cups dark chocolate chunks, divided

Flaky sea salt, for sprinkling

1 In a medium bowl, whisk together the flour, baking soda, and salt. Set aside.

2 Melt the butter in a light-colored saucepan over medium-low heat. Stir constantly as the butter melts and begins to foam and bubble, about 3 minutes. Continue cooking and stirring until you can see brown specks through the bubbles and foam and you smell a nutty aroma, about 5 minutes total. Remove from heat and strain with a fine mesh strainer into a small bowl to remove the larger brown bits, which can be bitter. Pour the browned liquid butter into the bowl of a stand mixer or a large bowl and cool to room temperature.

3 In the bowl of a stand mixer fitted with a paddle attachment or a large bowl with a hand mixer, beat the butter, brown sugar, and granulated sugar until combined. The mixture will look a little crumbly and wet. Add the eggs, one at a time, mixing after each addition, and then the vanilla extract and beat until everything is smooth and combined. Gradually add the flour mixture and mix on low speed until just combined. With a spatula, fold in 1¼ cups of the chocolate chunks, setting aside ¼ cup for finishing. Cover the dough and place it in the refrigerator to chill for 30 minutes.

4 When you're ready to bake, preheat your oven to 350°F. Line two baking sheets with parchment paper.

5 Form the dough into 3-tablespoon-size lumps and place 6 cookies on each baking sheet, about 3 inches apart.

6 Bake each batch, one baking sheet at a time, for 12 to 14 minutes, rotating the baking sheet halfway through, until the cookies are set and golden on the bottom. Transfer the baking sheet to a wire rack. While the cookies are still warm, press some of the reserved chocolate chunks into each one and sprinkle with sea salt. Cool the cookies completely before serving or storing.

Chocolate M&M'S COOKIES

Without a doubt, our family's all-time favorite candy is M&M's. We always keep a bag in the fridge. And let's be real, can you even have a movie night without M&M's? These cookies double down on rich chocolate flavor with a satisfying candy crunch. My tip: Save a few M&M's to place on top to really showcase this delicious treat. —J

3 cups all-purpose flour

⅔ cup unsweetened cocoa powder

1 teaspoon baking soda

1 teaspoon salt

1 cup unsalted butter, room temperature

1 cup light brown sugar, packed

1 cup granulated sugar

2 large eggs, room temperature

½ cup milk (2% or whole), room temperature

2 teaspoons vanilla extract

1 cup M&M's, divided

1 In a medium bowl, whisk together the flour, cocoa powder, baking soda, and salt. Set aside.

2 In the bowl of a stand mixer fitted with a paddle attachment or a large bowl with a hand mixer, beat the butter until creamy. Add the brown sugar and granulated sugar and beat until light and fluffy, 2 to 3 minutes. Add the eggs one at a time, mixing after each addition, then the milk, and the vanilla extract, mixing for 1 to 2 minutes, until well blended. Gradually add the dry ingredients to the wet ingredients and mix on low until just combined, scraping down the sides of the bowl as needed. With a spatula, fold in half of the M&M's, saving the other half for finishing. Cover the dough and let chill in the refrigerator for at least 1 hour.

3 When you're ready to bake, preheat your oven to 350°F. Line two baking sheets with parchment paper.

4 Using a cookie scoop or spoon, form the dough into golf ball–size balls. Place them on the prepared baking sheets 2 inches apart.

5 Bake each batch, one baking sheet at a time, for 10 to 12 minutes, rotating the baking sheet halfway through, until the edges begin to set. Remove each baking sheet from the oven and place on a wire rack. While the cookies are still slightly warm, add the extra M&M's to the tops, one by one. This gives the cookies a more polished, professional look. Cool the cookies completely before serving or storing.

ANGELA *and* ISABEL, professional taste testers

EGGNOG COOKIES

I love the first sip of eggnog at a holiday party! It's like an instant burst of holiday cheer: rich, creamy, and full of warm spices. But one sip is usually all I can handle. That's why these Eggnog Cookies are so perfect. They capture all that festive warmth into a light, sweet bite. It's the taste of eggnog in cookie form—just right for the season! —**A**

For the cookies

3½ cups all-purpose flour

1½ teaspoons baking powder

½ teaspoon salt

1 teaspoon ground cinnamon

2½ teaspoons ground nutmeg, divided

¼ teaspoon ground cloves

1 cup unsalted butter, softened

¾ cup granulated sugar, divided

½ cup light brown sugar, packed

2 large eggs, room temperature

1 teaspoon vanilla extract

½ teaspoon dark rum or rum extract (optional)

½ cup eggnog, room temperature

For the glaze

1½ cups powdered sugar

1 to 2 tablespoons eggnog

1 Make the cookies: In a medium bowl, whisk together the flour, baking powder, salt, cinnamon, ½ teaspoon of nutmeg, and the cloves. Set aside.

2 In the bowl of a stand mixer fitted with a paddle attachment or a large bowl with a hand mixer, beat the butter until creamy. Add ½ cup of granulated sugar and the brown sugar and beat until light and fluffy, about 2 to 3 minutes. Add the eggs one at a time, mixing after each addition, then the vanilla extract and, if using, the rum, mixing for 1 to 2 minutes, until well blended.

3 Gradually add half the flour mixture to the wet ingredients and mix on low until just combined, scraping down the sides of the bowl as needed. Pour in the eggnog and give it another good mix. Add the remaining flour mixture and mix again until just combined. The dough will be soft and sticky. Cover the dough and let it chill in the refrigerator for at least an hour.

4 When you're ready to bake, preheat your oven to 350°F. Line two baking sheets with parchment paper.

5 In a small bowl, whisk together the remaining granulated sugar and nutmeg. Using a cookie scoop or spoon, form the dough into golf ball–size balls. Roll the balls in the sugar and nutmeg mixture and place on the prepared baking sheets 2 inches apart.

6 Bake each batch, one baking sheet at a time, for 11 to 12 minutes, rotating the baking sheet halfway through, until they're a light golden brown on the bottom. Transfer to a wire rack to cool completely before you add the glaze.

7 Make the glaze: In a small bowl, whisk together the powdered sugar and eggnog until the mixture is thick yet pourable. Drizzle over the cookies. Get creative with designs, or add some sprinkles if you like! Let the glaze harden completely, about 30 minutes, before storing.

CINNAMON ROLL COOKIES

Get ready for compliments galore when you whip up these adorable cinnamon roll cookies! They have all the mouthwatering taste of a traditional cinnamon roll but in an easy-to-eat cookie shape. And hey, if you decide to sneak a few for breakfast, we won't tell!

For the cookies

2½ cups all-purpose flour, plus more for dusting

½ teaspoon ground cinnamon

½ teaspoon salt

¼ teaspoon baking powder

¾ cup unsalted butter, softened

½ cup light brown sugar, packed

½ cup granulated sugar

2 large eggs, room temperature

1 teaspoon vanilla extract

For the filling

¼ cup light brown sugar

1 tablespoon ground cinnamon

⅛ teaspoon salt

3 tablespoons unsalted butter

For the glaze

1 cup powdered sugar

1 tablespoon milk (2% or whole)

1 teaspoon vanilla extract

1 Make the cookies: In a medium bowl, whisk together the flour, cinnamon, salt, and baking powder. Set aside.

2 In the bowl of a stand mixer fitted with a paddle attachment or a large bowl with a hand mixer, beat the butter until creamy. Add the brown sugar and granulated sugar and beat until light and fluffy, about 2 to 3 minutes. Add the eggs one at a time, mixing after each addition and then the vanilla extract, mixing for 1 to 2 minutes, until the dough has an even consistency. Turn the mixer to low, add the flour mixture, and mix until just combined, scraping down the sides of the bowl as needed. Set aside.

3 Make the filling: Mix the brown sugar, cinnamon, and salt in a small bowl and set aside. In a separate small bowl, melt the butter in the microwave and set aside to cool while you roll out the dough.

4 Divide the dough in half. On a lightly floured surface, use a floured rolling pin to roll each half into an 8-by-5-inch rectangle about ¼ inch thick. Spread the butter over both rectangles, leaving a small border at the edges. Sprinkle the buttered area with the cinnamon sugar/salt mixture.

ISABEL *gets*
baking tips
from Nene.

5 Starting on the long side, roll the dough up tightly, making two 8-inch logs with cinnamon spirals. If the dough cracks, smooth it out with your fingers. Wrap each log in plastic wrap and chill for at least 3 hours in the refrigerator.

6 When you're ready to bake, preheat your oven to 350°F. Line two baking sheets with parchment paper.

7 You can roll the cookie logs around a bit after chilling to get a rounded edge again, because the logs will go a little flat on the bottom as they chill. This will also help keep the seal. Slice each log into ½-inch-thick cookies and place on the prepared baking sheets, spiral side up.

8 Bake each batch, one baking sheet at a time, for 9 to 10 minutes, rotating the baking sheet halfway through, until the edges are lightly browned. Remove from the oven and cool completely on a wire rack before adding the glaze.

9 **Make the glaze:** In a small bowl, whisk together the powdered sugar, milk, and vanilla extract. Add another tablespoon of milk, if needed, to thin out the glaze. You're looking for a thick drizzle consistency. Drizzle the glaze over the cookies using a piping bag or a spoon. Let it harden for about 1 hour before serving.

Cinnamon
Roll Cookies,
page 164

Edible COOKIE DOUGH BALLS

We've all done it, and some of us still do (looking at you, Angela). But let's face it, eating raw cookie dough, no matter how delicious, comes with risks. Raw eggs and uncooked flour are definite no-nos. This recipe, however, lets you indulge without worry. Enjoy it straight from the fridge, mix it into ice cream, or get creative with your favorite flavors. —**J**

1 cup all-purpose flour

½ cup unsalted butter, room temperature

¾ cups light brown sugar, packed

1½ teaspoons vanilla extract

½ teaspoon salt

1 to 2 tablespoons milk (2% or whole)

½ cup mini chocolate chips

1 Preheat your oven to 350°F. Line a baking sheet with parchment paper.

2 Sprinkle the flour onto the baking sheet in an even layer. Bake for 10 minutes. Remove from the oven and allow to cool completely, about 15 minutes.

3 In the bowl of a stand mixer fitted with a paddle attachment or a large bowl with a hand mixer, beat the butter until creamy. Add the brown sugar and vanilla extract and beat until light and fluffy, 2 to 3 minutes. Turn the mixer to low, add the cooled flour and salt, and mix until just combined, scraping down the sides of the bowl as needed. It may look a little crumbly, but that is okay. Add the milk, adjusting the quantity to achieve the perfect cookie dough consistency. With a spatula, fold in the mini chocolate chips.

4 Using a cookie scoop or a spoon, scoop 1½-tablespoon balls and place them on a large plate or baking sheet. Cover the dough balls loosely with plastic wrap and refrigerate until firm and chilled.

PECAN PIE COOKIES

My favorite nut, besides Ange (ha ha), is pecans. Sorry about the dad joke. But seriously, I love pecans, especially in pecan pie! I know Angela has shared about her grandparents' pecan trees, and I want you to know that to this day, Angela's mom sends us home with a huge zip-lock bag full of pecans every time we visit her family in Texas. These cookies capture the best parts of a classic pecan pie in a bite-size cookie and give you all the flavor of a classic pecan pie with way less effort. Personally, I love to make these cookies in the fall, but you can't go wrong any time of the year! —**J**

For the cookies

2 cups all-purpose flour

1 teaspoon cinnamon

1 teaspoon baking powder

½ teaspoon salt

¾ cup unsalted butter, softened

¾ cup light brown sugar, packed

1 large egg, room temperature

1 teaspoon vanilla extract

For the filling

⅔ cup chopped pecans

⅓ cup light brown sugar, packed

2 tablespoons heavy whipping cream

2 tablespoons maple syrup

½ teaspoon almond extract

1 Make the cookies: In a medium bowl, whisk together the flour, cinnamon, baking powder, and salt. Set aside.

2 In the bowl of a stand mixer fitted with a paddle attachment or a large bowl with a hand mixer, beat the butter until creamy. Add the brown sugar and beat until light and fluffy, 2 to 3 minutes. Add the egg and then the vanilla extract, mixing for 1 to 2 minutes, until well combined. Gradually add half the flour mixture and mix on low until just combined, scraping down the sides of the bowl as needed. Add the remaining flour mixture and mix again until just combined. Cover the dough with plastic wrap and let it chill in the refrigerator for at least an hour.

3 **Make the filling:** In a medium bowl, stir together the pecans, brown sugar, cream, maple syrup, and almond extract until well combined.

4 When you're ready to bake, preheat your oven to 350°F. Line two baking sheets with parchment paper.

5 Using a cookie scoop or spoon, form the dough into golf ball–size balls. Place them on the prepared baking sheets 2 inches apart. Using the back of a tablespoon or your thumb, make a well in the center of the dough balls. Fill each cookie well with 1½ teaspoons of the pecan pie filling.

6 Bake each batch, one baking sheet at a time, for 11 to 12 minutes, rotating the baking sheet halfway through, until the edges of the cookies are golden brown. Some of the filling might spill out over the edges of the cookies. Transfer to a wire rack and let cool completely before storing.

GINGERBREAD COOKIES

Every holiday season, we make sure to dedicate at least two days to cookie making and decorating, and it's always a blast. The spicy, warm flavor of gingerbread never fails to get us into the holiday spirit. It's always so much fun seeing the different versions of gingerbread people we create—some sad, some happy, some just plain weird (thanks, Cade!). This recipe won't give you ultracrisp gingerbread; instead, you'll get a softer, perfectly balanced cookie that you'll actually want to eat. It's a fun holiday activity for the whole family, and the cookies can be enjoyed for weeks or given as gifts.

2¾ cups all-purpose flour, plus more for dusting

2 teaspoons ground ginger

1 teaspoon ground cinnamon

½ teaspoon ground nutmeg

½ teaspoon ground cloves

½ teaspoon baking powder

½ teaspoon baking soda

½ teaspoon salt

¼ teaspoon ground white pepper

½ cup unsalted butter, room temperature

⅔ cup granulated sugar

½ cup unsulfured molasses

1 large egg, room temperature

1 teaspoon vanilla extract

1 In a medium bowl, whisk together the flour, ginger, cinnamon, nutmeg, cloves, baking powder, baking soda, salt, and white pepper. Set aside.

2 In the bowl of a stand mixer fitted with a paddle attachment or a large bowl with a hand mixer, beat the butter until creamy. Add the sugar and beat until light and fluffy, 2 to 3 minutes. Add the molasses, egg, and vanilla extract, beating for about 2 minutes, until well combined. Gradually add the flour mixture and mix on low until just combined, scraping down the sides of the bowl as needed. The dough will be sticky.

3 Scoop the dough onto a piece of plastic wrap and wrap it tightly. Shape it into a flat disk and chill in the refrigerator for at least 3 hours before rolling it out.

4 When you're ready to bake, preheat your oven to 375°F. Line two baking sheets with parchment paper.

5 On a floured surface, roll out the chilled dough to about ¼ inch thickness. Use cookie cutters to cut out shapes and place them on the prepared baking sheets. You can reroll the leftover dough scraps a few times and cut out more cookies.

6 Bake each batch, one baking sheet at a time, for 8 to 10 minutes, rotating the baking sheet halfway through, or until the edges are a deeper brown. Transfer the cookies to a wire rack and let them cool completely, especially if you'll be decorating them. Decorate the cooled cookies with Foolproof Royal Icing (page 193) or a glaze if you'd like.

Marbled MINT CHOCOLATE COOKIES

We stumbled across this recipe while scrambling to make a St. Patrick's Day dessert for the kids' school. I didn't have the time to decorate sugar cookies but needed something festive that wouldn't melt (we do live in Los Angeles, after all). I had made a vanilla version of this cookie before and it was fantastic, so I thought, why not add some flavor and color and put them together? And voilà, the Marbled Mint Chocolate Cookie was born! Imagine a pinwheel of rich chocolate, refreshing peppermint, and creamy vanilla, all combined together and the coarse sugar on top adds the perfect crunch. **–J**

3 cups all-purpose flour

½ teaspoon baking soda

½ teaspoon cream of tartar

½ teaspoon salt

1 cup unsalted butter, softened

1½ cups granulated sugar

2 large eggs, room temperature

1 teaspoon vanilla extract

2 to 4 teaspoons milk (2% or whole), divided

1 teaspoon peppermint extract

Green food coloring

2 tablespoons cocoa powder

Coarse sugar, for rolling

1 In a medium bowl, whisk together the flour, baking soda, cream of tartar, and salt. Set aside.

2 In the bowl of a stand mixer fitted with a paddle attachment or a large bowl with a hand mixer, beat the butter until creamy. Add the sugar and beat for 2 to 3 minutes, until light and fluffy. Add the eggs one at a time, mixing after each addition, and then the vanilla extract and mix until well combined. Gradually add half the flour mixture and mix on low until just combined, scraping down the sides of the bowl as needed. Add the remaining flour mixture and mix again until just combined.

3 Divide the dough into three equal portions, placing each in a separate medium bowl.

4 To the first bowl, add 1 teaspoon of milk, the peppermint extract, and a few drops of the green food coloring. Using a small spatula or spoon, mix thoroughly until the dough is uniformly green. Add a bit more milk if it seems too thick.

Recipe Continues

5 To the second bowl, stir in 1 teaspoon of milk and the cocoa powder. Using a small spatula or a spoon, mix thoroughly until the dough is smooth and evenly colored. If needed, add a touch more milk to achieve the desired consistency.

6 Leave the third bowl as is.

7 Cover each bowl of dough with plastic wrap and chill in the refrigerator for about 1 hour.

8 When you're ready to bake, preheat your oven to 350°F. Line two baking sheets with parchment paper.

9 Take a ⅔-tablespoon piece of dough from each of the bowls (vanilla, cocoa, and mint) and roll them into a golf ball–size ball, ensuring that all three colors are visible and your cookie contains 2 tablespoons of dough.

10 Add coarse sugar to a small bowl and roll each dough ball in it to coat. Place the balls on the prepared baking sheets, about 2 inches apart. Bake each batch, one baking sheet at a time, for 11 to 12 minutes, rotating the baking sheet halfway through, until the edges are very slightly browned. Remove from the oven and allow to cool completely on a wire rack before serving or storing.

No-Bake CHOCOLATE DROPS

These delicious No-Bake Chocolate Drops are straight from my Grandma Snyder's own cookbook, "Glenna's Favorites." Packed with rich chocolate, creamy peanut butter, and hearty oats, they are some of our favorite quick treats. While they do require some stovetop time and careful attention, they're quick to make and so good. I've updated the recipe a bit to make it easier to follow, but a big thank-you to my sweet grandma for preserving these recipes for our family. —**J**

½ cup unsalted butter

½ cup milk (2% or whole)

2 cups granulated sugar

½ cup unsweetened cocoa powder

½ teaspoon salt

½ cup creamy peanut butter

1 teaspoon vanilla extract

3 cups quick-cooking oats

1 Lay a large piece of parchment or wax paper on a smooth surface. This will serve as the area for your chocolate drops to cool and harden.

2 In a medium saucepan over medium heat, combine the butter, milk, sugar, cocoa powder, and salt. Whisk the mixture constantly until it reaches a rolling boil. Allow to boil for 1 minute, whisking. This process is key to achieving the correct consistency.

3 Remove the saucepan from the heat and stir in the peanut butter and vanilla extract with a spatula until the peanut butter is fully melted and the mixture is uniform. Quickly fold in the oats until they are thoroughly coated with the chocolate mixture.

4 Using a spoon or cookie scoop, portion 1-tablespoon spoonfuls of the mixture onto the prepared parchment or wax paper. Be careful, as the mixture will be quite hot. Let the chocolate drops cool and set at room temperature, 30 minutes to 1 hour, until firm. Store any leftovers in an airtight container at room temperature, or refrigerate if your kitchen is warm.

GRANDMA SNYDER *with her* COOKBOOK.

LEMON *Meltaway* COOKIES

Angela and Isabel love lemon desserts so I am always brainstorming new lemon treats for them. They love these Lemon Meltaway Cookies. Packed with zesty lemon flavor and finished with a tangy lemon glaze, they melt in your mouth. Thanks to a magic combination of cornstarch and powdered sugar, these cookies are amazingly light and tender. **—J**

For the cookies

1 cup all-purpose flour

2 teaspoons cornstarch

½ teaspoon salt

½ cup unsalted butter, softened

½ cup powdered sugar

1 large egg yolk, room temperature

1 tablespoon lemon zest, plus more for sprinkling

For the glaze

1 cup powdered sugar

1 tablespoon fresh lemon juice

1 Make the cookies: In a medium bowl, whisk together the flour, cornstarch, and salt. Set aside.

2 In the bowl of a stand mixer fitted with a paddle attachment or a large bowl with a hand mixer, beat the butter until creamy. Add the powdered sugar and beat until light and fluffy, 2 to 3 minutes. Add the egg yolk and lemon zest and mix until well blended, about 1 minute. Gradually add half the flour mixture and mix on low until just combined, scraping down the sides of the bowl as needed. Add the remaining flour mixture and beat just until the dough comes together. Cover the dough with plastic wrap and place in the fridge for at least 30 minutes to chill.

3 When you're ready to bake, preheat your oven to 350°F. Line two baking sheets with parchment paper.

4 Using a cookie scoop or spoon, scoop the dough into 1½-tablespoon-size lumps and form into Ping-Pong ball–size balls. Place them on the baking sheets at least 2 inches apart. Using the palm of your hand or the bottom of a glass, gently flatten the dough balls into circles.

5 Bake each batch, one baking sheet at a time, for 8 to 10 minutes, rotating the baking sheet halfway through, until the edges start to turn golden brown. Transfer to a wire rack and cool completely.

6 Make the glaze: In a medium bowl, whisk together the powdered sugar and half of the lemon juice. Adjust the thickness with more lemon juice if needed until the glaze is smooth and thick but still pourable. Spoon a bit of glaze onto each cookie and spread to the edges. Sprinkle with lemon zest. Let the cookies rest for 1 to 2 hours for the glaze to set before serving or storing.

Iced OATMEAL COOKIES

When I was a kid, my friend's mom always bought iced oatmeal cookies that came in a bag, and we would demolish them in no time. I knew I had to try to make my own version for my kids. I have to say, my recipe is even better than the store-bought cookie I grew up with. This cookie is soft and delicious, with a hint of cinnamon and topped with a sweet glaze. —**J**

For the cookies

1 cup old-fashioned rolled oats

1 cup all-purpose flour

1 teaspoon ground cinnamon

¼ teaspoon ground nutmeg

½ teaspoon baking powder

¼ teaspoon baking soda

½ teaspoon salt

½ cup unsalted butter, softened

½ cup light brown sugar, packed

¼ cup granulated sugar

1 large egg, room temperature

1 teaspoon vanilla extract

For the icing

¾ cup powdered sugar

¼ teaspoon vanilla extract

2 teaspoons milk (2% or whole)

1 **Make the cookies:** Pulse the oats in a food processor or a strong blender 2 to 3 times until they are a mix of fine and coarse bits. In a large bowl, whisk together the oats, flour, cinnamon, nutmeg, baking powder, baking soda, and salt. Set aside.

2 In the bowl of a stand mixer fitted with a paddle attachment or a large bowl with a hand mixer, beat the butter until creamy. Add the brown sugar and granulated sugar and beat until light and fluffy, 2 to 3 minutes. Add the egg and vanilla extract and mix until blended. Gradually add the oatmeal mixture and mix on low until just combined, scraping down the sides of the bowl as needed. Chill the dough in the refrigerator for at least 2 hours.

3 When you're ready to bake, preheat your oven to 350°F. Line two baking sheets with parchment paper.

4 Using a cookie scoop or a spoon, form the dough into golf ball–size balls. Place them on the prepared baking sheet 2 inches apart. Bake each batch, one baking sheet at a time, for 10 to 12 minutes, rotating the baking sheet halfway through, until the edges are golden brown. Flatten the tops of the cookies slightly with a spatula immediately after baking so they will hold the glaze better. Cool completely on a wire rack.

5 **Make the icing:** In a medium bowl, whisk together the powdered sugar, the vanilla extract, and half the milk. Gradually add the remaining milk until the glaze reaches a smooth, thick consistency like toothpaste. Holding the edge of each cooled cookie, dip the top into the glaze to coat. Let the cookies set for 1 to 2 hours before serving or storing.

Make this!

If you don't have a food processor, you can substitute quick-cooking oats for the old-fashioned rolled oats. When using quick-cooking oats, measure the same amount as you would for old-fashioned oats and mix them into the dough without the pulsing step.

Lofthouse-Style SUGAR COOKIES

Back when our kids were little, a trip to the grocery store bakery often ended with a few Lofthouse-Style Sugar Cookies as a reward for good behavior. They loved the bright frosting and sprinkles; it was like a minicelebration every time. Now, with this recipe, we bring that same bakery magic home!

For the cookies

3 cups all-purpose flour, plus more for dusting

1 tablespoon cornstarch

½ teaspoon baking soda

½ teaspoon baking powder

½ teaspoon salt

½ cup unsalted butter, softened

¾ cup sour cream, room temperature

1 cup granulated sugar

1 large egg, room temperature

1 large egg yolk, room temperature

1 teaspoon vanilla extract

For the buttercream

½ cup unsalted butter, softened

½ teaspoon vanilla extract

½ teaspoon salt

2½ cups powdered sugar

1 to 2 tablespoons heavy whipping cream

Sprinkles (optional)

1 **Make the cookies:** In a medium bowl, whisk together the flour, cornstarch, baking soda, baking powder, and salt. Set aside.

2 In the bowl of a stand mixer fitted with a paddle attachment or a large bowl with a hand mixer, beat the butter and sour cream until creamy. Add the sugar and beat until light and fluffy, 2 to 3 minutes. Add the egg, egg yolk, and vanilla extract and mix for 1 to 2 minutes, until well combined. Gradually add half of the flour mixture and mix on low until just combined, scraping down the sides of the bowl as needed. Add the remaining flour mixture and beat until the dough just comes together.

3 Divide the dough into 2 equal-size discs. Wrap tightly in plastic wrap and refrigerate for at least 2 hours.

4 When you're ready to bake, preheat your oven to 375°F. Line two baking sheets with parchment paper.

5 Working in batches, transfer the chilled dough to a work surface dusted with flour. Roll out the dough to ¼-inch thickness using a rolling pin. Cut out the cookies with a 2½- or 3-inch circle cutter and place them on the prepared baking sheets 2 inches apart.

6 Bake each batch, one baking sheet a time, for 7 to 8 minutes, rotating the baking sheet halfway through, until the edges are very slightly golden. Let the cookies cool on the baking sheet for 5 minutes before transferring them to a wire rack to cool completely.

7 **Make the buttercream:** In the bowl of a stand mixer fitted with a paddle attachment or a large bowl with a hand mixer, beat the butter until creamy. Add the vanilla extract and salt and beat until combined. On low speed, slowly add the powdered sugar. The mixture might look a bit lumpy at first. Pour in a bit of the heavy whipping cream and mix until it's smooth and thick. Turn the speed to medium high and beat for another 1 to 2 minutes, until light and fluffy.

8 Pipe the cooled cookies with buttercream or neatly frost them with a butter knife. Decorate with sprinkles if desired. Let the cookies sit for about 1 hour to let the buttercream harden before serving or storing.

Pumpkin SNICKERDOODLES

Snickerdoodles were one of the first recipes, along with my now-neighborhood-famous decorated sugar cookies (see page 191), that I truly mastered. My version is soft, fluffy, cakelike, and absolutely delicious. My family is obsessed with anything pumpkin flavored, so I decided to adapt my original snickerdoodle recipe with a pumpkin spice twist. Not only do they taste fantastic, but they maintain their soft, cakelike, melt-in-the-mouth texture. —**J**

For the cookies

1¾ cups all-purpose flour

2 teaspoons pumpkin pie spice

1 teaspoon cream of tartar

½ teaspoon baking soda

¼ teaspoon salt

½ cup unsalted butter, softened

½ cup light brown sugar, packed

½ cup granulated sugar

1 large egg yolk, room temperature

¼ cup pumpkin puree

For the topping

2 tablespoons granulated sugar

1 teaspoon ground cinnamon

1 teaspoon pumpkin pie spice

1 **Make the cookies:** In a medium bowl, whisk together the flour, pumpkin pie spice, cream of tartar, baking soda, and salt. Set aside.

2 In the bowl of a stand mixer fitted with a paddle attachment or a large bowl with a hand mixer, beat the butter until creamy. Add the brown sugar and granulated sugar and beat until light and fluffy, 2 to 3 minutes. Add the egg yolk and pumpkin puree, mixing for 1 to 2 minutes, until well combined. Gradually add half the flour mixture and mix on low until just incorporated, scraping down the sides of the bowl as needed. Add the remaining flour mixture and mix again until just combined. Cover the dough and chill in the refrigerator for about 1 hour.

3 When you're ready to bake, preheat your oven to 350°F. Line two baking sheets with parchment paper.

4 **Make the topping:** In a small bowl, mix together the sugar, cinnamon, and pumpkin pie spice. Using a cookie scoop or spoon, scoop the dough into golf ball–size balls. Roll them through the spice mixture until well coated. Place them on the baking sheets about 2 inches apart.

5 Bake each batch, one baking sheet at a time, for 11 to 12 minutes, rotating the baking sheet halfway through, until the edges are a light golden brown. Allow to cool on the baking sheet for 10 minutes before transferring to a wire rack.

Soft GINGER COOKIES *with* BROWN BUTTER ICING

These are inspired by my great-grandma's ginger cookies, a recipe passed down through the generations. I've put my spin on it by using butter instead of margarine and adding browned butter to the icing for extra flavor. The cookies are perfectly soft, with rich molasses and just the right blend of ginger, cinnamon, and cloves. And the icing? It's rich and sweet with a hint of nuttiness that makes these cookies irresistible. Even at ninety-six years old, my grandma still bakes the original version during our holiday visits. These cookies are more than just a treat; they're part of our family history, filled with love and warmth. **—J**

For the icing

1 cup unsalted butter

3 cups powdered sugar

1 tablespoon milk, plus more as needed

2 teaspoons vanilla extract

For the cookies

2¼ cups all-purpose flour

2 teaspoons ground ginger

1 teaspoon ground cinnamon

1 teaspoon baking powder

½ teaspoon baking soda

½ teaspoon salt

¼ cup milk (2% or whole), room temperature

1 teaspoon apple cider vinegar

2 tablespoons water

½ cup unsalted butter, softened

2 tablespoons canola oil

½ cup light brown sugar, packed

½ cup unsulfured molasses

1 large egg, room temperature

Ground ginger, for dusting (optional)

1 **Make the icing:** Melt the butter in a small light-colored saucepan over medium-low heat. Cook for about 3 minutes, stirring constantly, until the butter foams and bubbles. Continue cooking until you can see brown specks through the bubbles and foam. Remove from the heat and, using a fine-mesh strainer, strain into a small bowl, discarding the solids. Place in the refrigerator for 30 minutes to 1 hour, until solid. Remove from the refrigerator about 30 minutes before using to soften.

2 In a medium bowl, beat the softened browned butter and until creamy. Add the powdered sugar and beat until combined. Add the milk and vanilla extract and mix until smooth. Add more milk if needed to reach a spreadable consistency. Cover and set aside until you are ready to frost the cookies.

VISITING family in Kansas *over* *the* HOLIDAYS

3 **Make the cookies:** In a second medium bowl, whisk together the flour, ginger, cinnamon, baking powder, baking soda, and salt. Set aside.

4 In a third medium bowl, stir together the milk, vinegar, and water. Set aside.

5 In the bowl of a stand mixer fitted with a paddle attachment or a large bowl with a hand mixer, beat the butter and oil until creamy. Add the brown sugar and beat until light and fluffy, 2 to 3 minutes. Add the molasses and egg and mix for 1 to 2 minutes, until well combined. Gradually add half the flour mixture and mix on low until just combined, scraping down the sides of the bowl as needed. Beat in the milk mixture, then add the remaining flour mixture and mix again until just combined. Cover the dough with plastic wrap and chill in the refrigerator for at least 1 hour before baking.

6 When you're ready to bake, preheat your oven to 350°F. Line two baking sheets with parchment paper.

7 Using a cookie scoop or spoon, form the dough into golf ball–size balls. Place them on a baking sheet about 2 inches apart.

8 Bake each batch, one baking sheet at a time, for 11 to 12 minutes, rotating the sheet halfway through, until the cookies are deep golden brown on the bottom. Let cool for about 5 minutes on the pan, then transfer to a wire rack. While the cookies are still a little warm, frost them with the icing using a butter knife. Dust with extra ground ginger if desired.

Soft Ginger
Cookies with
Brown Butter
Icing, page 184

Stacked S'MORES BROWNIE COOKIES

Our family has a thing for s'mores—we love gathering around the backyard
fire pit every summer to make them. One year, Jack even had a s'mores birthday party!
This recipe yields only eight of these treats because each one is a towering delight,
stacked with layers of chocolate cookie, chocolate chip graham cracker, fudgy
brownie, and toasted marshmallow. When you want a big treat for yourself or one
that is perfect for sharing, just pop them into the microwave for a few seconds, and
you'll have a warm, gooey dessert that's perfect for any s'mores lover.

For the cookie dough

1¼ cups all-purpose flour

½ teaspoon baking soda

½ teaspoon salt

½ cup unsalted butter,
softened

¾ cup light brown sugar,
packed

¼ cup granulated sugar

1 large egg, room
temperature

2 teaspoons vanilla
extract

⅓ cup cocoa powder

1 tablespoon milk (2% or
whole)

⅓ cup graham cracker
crumbs

¼ cup chocolate chips

For the brownie batter

¼ cup semisweet
chocolate chips

2 tablespoons unsalted
butter

1 large egg yolk

2 tablespoons brown
sugar

2 tablespoons flour

For assembly

4 large marshmallows,
cut in half

1 **Make the cookie dough:** In a medium bowl, whisk
together the flour, baking soda, and salt. Set aside.

2 In the bowl of a stand mixer fitted with a paddle
attachment or a large bowl with a hand mixer, beat
the butter until creamy. Add the brown sugar and
granulated sugar and beat until light and fluffy,
2 to 3 minutes. Add the egg and then the vanilla
extract, mixing for 1 to 2 minutes, until well combined.
Gradually add half of the flour mixture and mix on
low until just combined, scraping down the sides of
the bowl as needed. Add the remaining flour mixture
and mix again until just combined.

3 Divide the dough into two portions, about
60 percent for one and 40 percent for the other.
Place each portion in its own bowl.

4 With a wooden spoon or spatula, mix the cocoa
powder and milk into the larger portion of dough
until well combined.

5 Fold the graham cracker crumbs and chocolate
chips into the smaller portion of dough until well
combined.

Recipe Continues

6 Cover each bowl of dough with plastic wrap and refrigerate for about 30 minutes.

7 **Make the brownie batter:** In a medium microwave-safe bowl, microwave the chocolate chips together with the butter for 45 seconds at half power, then in 15-second increments at half power, stirring after each interval, until smooth. Let the chocolate mixture cool slightly, then whisk in the egg yolk, brown sugar, and flour.

8 When you're ready to bake, preheat your oven to 350°F. Line two baking sheets with parchment paper.

9 **Assemble the cookie:** Take both cookie doughs out of the refrigerator. Scoop a 2-tablespoon portion of the chocolate dough, roll it into a ball, place on the baking sheet, and flatten it with the palm of your hand.

10 Scoop a 1½-tablespoon portion of the graham cracker dough, stack it on top of the chocolate dough, and press them together gently.

11 With the back of a spoon, make a small well in the graham cracker dough and add 1 tablespoon of the brownie batter on top of each cookie stack. Repeat the process to make 8 cookies, placing 4 cookies on each baking sheet. Bake for 10 minutes.

12 Remove from the oven, place half a marshmallow on top of each cookie, and bake for another 3 to 4 minutes, until the brownie batter is set and the edges of the graham cracker dough turn a golden brown.

13 Remove from the oven and let cool on the baking sheet. If you like, lightly toast the marshmallow with a kitchen torch.

" OUR
FAMILY
has a thing
for S'MORES.

Rolled SUGAR COOKIES *with* FOOLPROOF ROYAL ICING

For over fifteen years, decorated sugar cookies have been my go-to for birthdays, school events, and special occasions. They are a bit of a time commitment to make, but seeing those finished cookies makes it all worth it. One of my favorite family traditions is decorating these cookies with Ange and the kids during the holidays. It's so much fun watching our kids' creativity shine and their skills improve (they can even tell the difference between flood and outline icing now!). It's become a special family activity, and who knows? You might just find a hidden passion as I did! —**J**

2½ **cups all-purpose flour, plus more for dusting**

⅛ **teaspoon baking powder**

½ **teaspoon salt**

¾ **cup unsalted butter, softened**

1 **cup granulated sugar**

2 **large eggs, room temperature**

½ **teaspoon vanilla extract**

Foolproof Royal Icing (page 193)

1 In a medium bowl, whisk together the flour, baking powder, and salt. Set aside.

2 In the bowl of a stand mixer fitted with a paddle attachment or a large bowl with a hand mixer, beat the butter until creamy. Add the sugar and beat until light and fluffy, 2 to 3 minutes. Add the eggs and then the vanilla extract, mixing for 1 to 2 minutes, until combined. Gradually add half the flour mixture and mix on low until just combined, scraping down the sides of the bowl as needed. Add the remaining flour mixture and mix again until just combined. The dough will be thick and sticky. Cover the dough with plastic wrap and refrigerate for at least 3 hours before baking.

3 When you're ready to bake, preheat the oven to 400°F. Line two baking sheets with parchment paper.

4 On a floured surface or silicone mat, use a floured rolling pin to roll out the dough to ¼-inch thickness. Use cookie cutters to cut the dough into shapes and place them on the prepared baking sheets. Gather any dough scraps and gently press them together. Reroll the scraps and cut out more cookies, but avoid doing this more than once as the dough will become tough.

5 Bake the cookies for 6 to 7 minutes, until the edges are just golden brown. Remove from the oven and allow the cookies to cool completely on a wire rack before decorating.

Recipe Continues

Foolproof Royal Icing

Makes 6 cups

1 (2-pound) bag powdered sugar

5 tablespoons meringue powder

¾ cup lukewarm water

1½ teaspoons almond extract

1 tablespoon light corn syrup

Spray bottle with water (optional)

1 In a large bowl, preferably the bowl of a stand mixer with a whisk attachment, whisk together the powdered sugar and meringue powder on low speed until combined.

2 In a small bowl, combine the lukewarm water and almond extract. With the mixer on its lowest speed, gradually pour the water-extract mixture into the powdered sugar mixture. The icing may look thick and lumpy, but continue adding lukewarm water until you reach a consistency like honey. Spray the edges of the bowl with water if there is extra powdered sugar there. Still mixing on low speed, drizzle in the corn syrup.

3 Increase the mixer speed to medium and mix for 1 minute, then ramp up to medium-high speed for 2 minutes to ensure that everything is thoroughly combined. The icing will start to gain volume and look silky and smooth. You can now thin the icing with more water from the spray bottle if needed.

4 Promptly transfer the icing to an airtight container until you're ready to add color and decorate. The icing will keep at room temperature until ready to use. If the icing begins to separate, just mix in the mixer for a few minutes until smooth again.

Make this!

To optimize your icing for outlining, aim for a toothpastelike consistency. For flood icing, you will need to thin the icing further with water, using the spray bottle to add a few sprays at a time until it reaches a smooth, honeylike consistency. Add gel food coloring to achieve your desired shade. Be sure to mix thoroughly. Transfer the outline and flood icing to squeeze bottles or piping bags for best results. I prefer using squeeze bottles for decorating, but you can use piping bags if you prefer.

Royal icing sets quickly when exposed to air. Always keep it covered when not in use to prevent it from drying out.

Brownies
and Bars

Homemade FUDGY BROWNIES

I know there are many different brownie recipes out there, but I'm picky and I wanted to make *the* best brownie. Now, some folks like them cakey, some are all about dark chocolate, and some (like Ange) swear by good old-fashioned box-mix brownies. So how do you know which way to go? Well, if you're a fan of fudgy brownies with a gooey middle, this recipe is for you. After countless tests with the kids and Ange as my trusty taste testers, I think I've nailed it. These brownies consistently get high praise (at least in our neighborhood) for being the fudgiest and best brownies in town. **—J**

1 cup semisweet chocolate chips

¾ cup unsalted butter

1 tablespoon unsweetened cocoa powder

3 large eggs, room temperature

1 cup granulated sugar

½ cup light brown sugar, packed

1 teaspoon vanilla extract

½ teaspoon salt

¾ cup all-purpose flour

Flaky sea salt, for topping (optional)

1 Preheat your oven to 350°F. Line a 9-inch-square baking pan with parchment paper, leaving a 1-inch overhang over two sides. Set aside.

2 In a medium microwave-safe bowl, microwave the chocolate chips together with the butter for 45 seconds at half power, then in 15-second increments at half power, stirring after each interval, until smooth. Stir in the cocoa powder until fully combined. Set aside.

3 In a large bowl, whisk the eggs with the granulated sugar and brown sugar until combined. Pour the warm chocolate mixture, vanilla extract, and salt into the egg mixture and whisk until blended. With a spatula, fold in the flour until the batter is lump free. Pour the batter into the prepared pan, tapping it on the counter a few times to release air bubbles on top.

4 Bake for 30 to 35 minutes, until the edges are set and a toothpick inserted comes out with just a few moist crumbs. Remove from the oven and allow to cool in the pan for at least 1 hour. Once the bars are completely cool, use the parchment paper to lift them out of the pan. Cut them into squares. Top with flaky sea salt, if desired, before serving.

BROOKIE BARS

These might be the perfect dessert. They combine a fudgy brownie and a chewy chocolate chip cookie. What is better than that? When I started baking these Brookie Bars, they became the only dessert our kids wanted. The trickiest part is layering the cookie dough on top of the brownie, but once you get the hang of it, you're set. **—J**

For the brownie layer

¼ cup all-purpose flour

¼ cup unsweetened cocoa powder

¼ teaspoon salt

¼ cup unsalted butter, melted and cooled to room temperature

⅛ cup vegetable oil

⅔ cup granulated sugar

1 large egg, room temperature

½ teaspoon vanilla extract

¼ cup semisweet mini chocolate chips

For the cookie layer

1 cup all-purpose flour

½ teaspoon baking powder

¼ teaspoon baking soda

¼ teaspoon salt

½ cup unsalted butter, softened

½ cup light brown sugar, packed

¼ cup granulated sugar

1 large egg, room temperature

1 teaspoon vanilla extract

½ cup semisweet mini chocolate chips, plus extra for topping

1 Make the brownie layer: Preheat your oven to 350°F. Line an 8-inch-square baking pan with parchment paper, leaving a 1-inch overhang over two sides. Set aside.

2 In a medium bowl, whisk together the flour, cocoa powder, and salt. Set aside.

3 In a large bowl, whisk together the butter, oil, and sugar until combined. Add the egg and vanilla extract and whisk until the mixture is uniform. Gently stir in the flour mixture into the wet ingredients until just combined. Using a spatula, fold in the mini chocolate chips. Transfer the batter to the prepared pan, smoothing it into an even layer. Set aside.

4 Make the cookie layer: In a medium bowl, whisk together the flour, baking powder, baking soda, and salt. Set aside.

5 In the bowl of a stand mixer fitted with a paddle attachment or a large bowl with a hand mixer, beat the butter, brown sugar, and granulated sugar until light and fluffy, 2 to 3 minutes. Add the egg and vanilla extract and mix until incorporated. Turn the mixer to low, slowly add the flour mixture, and mix until just combined, being careful not to overmix. Using a spatula, fold in the mini chocolate chips.

6 Using a large cookie scoop or spoon, distribute evenly-sized dollops of the dough across the surface of the brownie batter, then carefully spread the dough across the brownie layer until it's completely covered, making sure that the bottom layer of brownie batter is not visible.

7 Bake for 30 to 35 minutes, until the edges are set and browned and a toothpick inserted into the center comes out clean. Remove from the oven and sprinkle with a small handful of chocolate chips for a more professional look. Allow the bars to cool completely in the pan. Once the bars are completely cool, use the parchment paper to lift them out of the pan. Cut into squares.

Chewy OATMEAL CHOCOLATE CHIP BARS

These might be the most frequently made treat in our house. Everyone in the family loves them. They're perfect for lunchboxes or a midday snack, and they store well so they stay fresh for a long time. They're fantastic on their own, or hear me out: If you like to zhush up some plain ol' ice cream, crumble these bars on top! Plus, the recipe makes a big batch, so they are great for gift giving. I love taking these bars to teacher appreciation day at school. —**A**

1½ cups all-purpose flour

1 teaspoon ground cinnamon

1 teaspoon baking powder

½ teaspoon baking soda

½ teaspoon salt

1 cup unsalted butter, softened

1 cup light brown sugar, packed

½ cup granulated sugar

2 large eggs, room temperature

2 teaspoons vanilla extract

2 cups old-fashioned rolled oats

1 cup semisweet chocolate chips, divided

1 Preheat your oven to 350°F. Either grease a 13-by-9-inch baking dish or line it with parchment paper, leaving a 1-inch overhang over two sides. Set aside.

2 In a medium bowl, whisk together the flour, cinnamon, baking powder, baking soda, and salt. Set aside.

3 In the bowl of a stand mixer fitted with a paddle attachment or a large bowl with a hand mixer, beat the butter until creamy. Add the brown sugar and granulated sugar and continue beating until well combined. Add the eggs one at a time, mixing after each addition, and then the vanilla extract and beat on medium high until the mixture is smooth. Turn speed to low, add the flour mixture, and beat until just combined. Gently fold in the rolled oats and ¾ cup of chocolate chips. Spread the mixture evenly into the prepared baking dish. It will be sticky.

4 Bake for 30 to 35 minutes, until the edges are brown. Remove from the oven and, while still warm, evenly top with the remaining ¼ cup chocolate chips. Allow the bars to cool completely in the pan. Once the bars are completely cool, use the parchment paper to lift them out of the pan. Cut them into squares.

MILLIONAIRE BARS

In our family, we love a good candy bar, so these Twix-like dessert bars are a huge hit. They are layered to perfection with a crisp shortbread crust and a creamy caramel middle, then topped with a smooth chocolate finish. Sprinkle them with sea salt and serve. Guaranteed happiness! The caramel layer can be a bit tricky, so using store-bought caramels is a great way to simplify and save time.

For the shortbread layer

1 cup unsalted butter, softened

1 cup light brown sugar, packed

2 teaspoons vanilla extract

1 teaspoon salt

3 cups all-purpose flour

2 tablespoons milk (2% or whole)

For the caramel layer

2 (11-ounce) packages of caramels, unwrapped (I use Kraft caramels)

2 tablespoons heavy cream

For the chocolate layer

2 cups semisweet chocolate chunks or chips

1 teaspoon canola oil

Flaky sea salt

1 Make the shortbread: Preheat your oven to 325°F. Line a 13-by-9-inch glass dish with parchment paper leaving a 1-inch overhang over two sides, or spray with nonstick spray or cooking spray.

2 In the bowl of a stand mixer fitted with a paddle attachment or a large bowl with a hand mixer, beat the butter until creamy. Add the brown sugar, vanilla extract, and salt and continue beating until well combined. Add the flour and mix on low until the mixture is combined and crumbly. Gradually add the milk, mixing until the dough sticks together when you pinch it.

3 Add the dough to the prepared baking dish. Place a piece of parchment paper over the dough and press it down evenly with your hands to form a solid layer. You can also use a small, flat baking pan for this.

4 Bake for about 20 minutes, until the crust begins to brown at the edges. Let the shortbread cool on a wire rack as you prepare the caramel layer.

5 Make the caramel layer: In a small saucepan over low heat, gently melt the caramels and heavy cream, being careful that the caramels don't burn. Stir continuously with a silicone spatula or wooden spoon. This can take anywhere from 5 to 10 minutes. Low and slow is the mantra for melting caramels. Once the caramels are fully melted and smooth, pour the mixture over the cooled shortbread crust. Place in the refrigerator for about 1 hour to fully set.

6 Make the chocolate layer: In a medium microwave-safe medium bowl, microwave the chocolate together with the oil for 45 seconds at half power, then in 15-second increments at half power, stirring after each interval, until smooth. Spread the melted chocolate over the caramel layer. Smooth the top with a knife, spatula, or bench scraper, ensuring that it is evenly covered. Refrigerate for at least 1 hour, until the chocolate sets. Once the bars are cool, use the parchment paper to lift them out of the pan.

7 Cut into bars using a sharp knife. For cleaner cuts, dip your knife in hot water, wipe it dry with a clean towel, then slice the bars. Repeat this step between slices. This will help you cut through the chocolate layer without cracking it.

8 Sprinkle flaky sea salt over the top. Eat immediately, or store in the refrigerator until ready to serve. If stored in the refrigerator, let the bars come back to room temperature before eating.

Peanut Butter PRETZEL BARS

Hey, there, Angela here. If I had to award a Dundie to a recipe in our cookbook, this one would win "Best Bar" hands down (and no, Meredith, that does not mean booze). These bars are super easy to make and taste incredible. The crust is a combination of crunchy pretzels and creamy peanut butter topped with . . . wait for it . . . a layer of chocolate. Get out! Whip up a big batch, keep them in the fridge, and grab a bite whenever you want. —**A**

For the crust

4 cups mini pretzel twists

2 cups powdered sugar

¾ cup unsalted butter, melted

1 cup creamy peanut butter

For the topping

2 cups semisweet chocolate chips

⅓ cup creamy peanut butter

1 Make the crust: Line a 13-by-9-inch baking dish with parchment paper, leaving a 1-inch overhang on two sides. Set aside.

2 In a food processor, pulse the pretzels in short bursts until they reach a coarse, sandlike consistency. You could also put them into a resealable bag and crush with a rolling pin. You should have 2½ cups of crushed pretzels.

3 In a large bowl, mix together the crushed pretzels and powdered sugar using a fork until the pretzel pieces are coated in the sugar. Add the butter and stir until everything is well combined. It should look like moist sand and stick together when pressed between your thumb and forefinger.

4 In a medium microwave-safe bowl, microwave the peanut butter for 20 seconds at high power. It should look smooth and runny. Pour into the pretzel mixture and stir together to fully combine.

5 Transfer the mixture to the prepared baking dish. Use a piece of parchment paper to press it down firmly into the dish with your hands until it forms a solid, even layer. You can also use a small flat dish or a baking pan to press it down.

6 Make the topping: In a medium microwave-safe bowl, microwave the chocolate chips and peanut butter for 1 minute at half power, then in 15-second increments at half power, stirring after each interval, until smooth.

7 Spread the melted chocolate over the pretzel layer. Smooth the top with a knife, spatula, or bench scraper, ensuring that it is evenly covered. Cover the dish with plastic wrap and refrigerate for 1 to 2 hours to set the chocolate. Once the bar is cool and the chocolate is set, use the parchment paper to lift it out and cut it into squares. Store in the refrigerator until you're ready to serve.

Peanut Butter–Stuffed CHOCOLATE CHIP BLONDIES

These blondies are delicious. Our favorite part is the creamy peanut butter center. This is definitely not your average peanut butter dessert!

1 cup creamy peanut butter

¼ cup powdered sugar

2 cups all-purpose flour

1 teaspoon baking powder

1 teaspoon salt

¾ cup unsalted butter, melted and cooled to room temperature

2 cups light brown sugar, packed

2 large eggs, room temperature

2 teaspoons vanilla extract

⅔ cup semisweet chocolate chips, plus 3 tablespoons for topping

1 Line a 9-inch-square baking pan with parchment paper and leave a one-inch overhang on two sides. Set aside.

2 In a microwave-safe bowl, stir together the peanut butter and powdered sugar. Microwave at high power for 30 seconds, then in 15-second increments at high power, stirring after each interval, until smooth and pourable. Spread the mixture on the prepared baking pan and smooth to create an even layer. Freeze for 1 hour, until solid.

3 Using the parchment paper, lift it out of the baking pan. Cover with plastic wrap and place on a small baking sheet. Return to the freezer while preparing the blondie batter and allow the baking pan to come up to room temperature.

4 Preheat your oven to 350°F. Line the baking pan with a fresh piece of parchment paper, again leaving a 1-inch overhang over two sides. Set aside.

5 In a medium bowl, whisk together the flour, baking powder, and salt. Set aside.

6 In a large bowl, whisk together the butter and brown sugar. Add the eggs and vanilla extract and whisk until smooth. Add the flour mixture and, using a wooden spoon or spatula, stir until combined. Fold in the chocolate chips.

7 Scoop half of the blondie batter into the prepared pan, spreading it evenly to the edges. Retrieve the peanut butter layer from the freezer, remove the plastic wrap, and place on top of the batter. Cover the peanut butter layer with the remaining blondie batter, making sure that the peanut butter layer is fully covered.

8 Bake for 25 to 30 minutes, until the edges are set and golden. Remove from the oven and sprinkle with additional chocolate chips. Cool the blondies completely in the pan in the refrigerator. Once the blondies are completely cool, use the parchment paper to lift them from the pan. Cut them into squares.

BROWN SUGAR SQUARES

As a kid, I used to sneak spoonfuls of brown sugar straight from the pantry. I thought I had gotten away with it until one afternoon when my grandma told me that she had known all along but she'd figured a spoonful of brown sugar once in a while wouldn't hurt me, so she'd never said anything. This recipe is one of her specialties. She even included it in the cookbook she made to give family and friends. I asked her if I could share it with you, so here are Grandma Snyder's Brown Sugar Squares! —J

For the crust

½ cup unsalted butter, softened

½ cup light brown sugar, packed

1 cup all-purpose flour

For the filling

2 tablespoons all-purpose flour

½ teaspoon baking powder

¼ teaspoon salt

3 large eggs, room temperature

1 cup light brown sugar, packed

1 teaspoon vanilla extract

½ cup sweetened flaked coconut

1 cup chopped pecans

1 **Make the crust:** Preheat your oven to 300°F. Line an 8-inch-square baking pan with parchment paper, leaving a 1-inch overhang over two sides. Set aside.

2 In the bowl of a stand mixer fitted with a paddle attachment or a large bowl with a hand mixer, beat the butter until creamy. Add the brown sugar and continue beating until well combined. With a spatula, stir in the flour until the mixture is a crumbly consistency. Transfer the mixture to the prepared baking dish and pat down into an even layer.

3 Bake for 20 to 25 minutes, until light brown. Remove and set aside to cool.

4 Increase the oven temperature to 350°F while you prepare the filling.

5 **Make the filling:** In a small bowl, whisk together the flour, baking powder, and salt. Set aside.

6 In the bowl of a stand mixer fitted with a whisk attachment or a large bowl with a hand mixer, beat the eggs, brown sugar, and vanilla extract until combined. Add the flour mixture and mix until just combined, then fold in the coconut and pecans. Spread evenly over the baked crust.

7 Bake for 25 to 30 minutes, until the top is set. Transfer to a wire rack and cool completely. Once the bars are completely cool, use the parchment paper to lift them out of the pan. Cut them into squares.

RASPBERRY OAT BARS

I am constantly asking Josh to make me a dessert with raspberries as the main ingredient. So when our Uncle Gary sent us a few jars of his homemade raspberry preserves (they are next-level delicious), I turned to Josh and said, "Make this happen for me." And let me tell you, the man knocked it out of the park. The best part: They are super easy to make. Even if you don't have an Uncle Gary who sends you homemade raspberry preserves, you can grab a jar at the grocery store and make one of my all-time favorite desserts. —A

1½ cups all-purpose flour

1 cup old-fashioned rolled oats

½ cup granulated sugar

½ cup brown sugar, packed

½ teaspoon ground cinnamon

¼ teaspoon ground nutmeg

½ teaspoon salt

¾ cup unsalted butter, melted

1 teaspoon vanilla extract

1 cup raspberry preserves

1 Preheat the oven to 350°F. Line an 8-inch-square baking dish with parchment paper, leaving a 1-inch overhang on two sides. Set aside.

2 In a large bowl, combine the flour, oats, granulated sugar, brown sugar, cinnamon, nutmeg, and salt. Add the melted butter and vanilla extract and stir well until combined. Remove and reserve 1½ cups for the topping. Press the remaining mixture firmly into the bottom of the prepared baking dish in an even layer.

3 Bake for 10 minutes. Remove and allow to cool slightly. Once cool, spread the raspberry preserves evenly over it and sprinkle the reserved crumble evenly over the top. Return to the oven and bake for 30 to 35 minutes, until the crumb topping is lightly golden. Allow the bars to cool completely in the pan.

4 For optimal slicing, cover with plastic wrap and place in the refrigerator for 1 hour before cutting into squares. Once the bars are cool, use the parchment to lift them out of the pan. Cut them into squares.

" One of my all-time FAVORITE DESSERTS

Cakes and Cupcakes

Almond TEA CAKE

Almond Tea Cake offers a delicate balance of sweetness and nuttiness, and it looks so fancy without much effort! You can make your own almond paste or buy it from the store. Topped with sliced almonds and a brush of simple syrup, this cake not only is delicious but also looks beautiful on a table. I once made it for my book club meeting, and all anyone asked me about was this cake. (That was lucky for me, because I hadn't finished reading the book.) —**A**

1 cup cake flour

½ teaspoon baking powder

¼ teaspoon salt

8 ounces almond paste

¾ cup unsalted butter, softened

1 cup granulated sugar

3 large eggs, room temperature

1 tablespoon lemon zest

2 teaspoons almond extract

1½ cups sliced almonds

Powdered sugar, for dusting

Berries and whipped cream, for topping (optional)

1 Preheat your oven to 325°F. Line the bottom of a 9-inch springform pan with a parchment paper circle. Grease the inside of the pan with nonstick spray, cooking spray, or butter. Set aside.

2 In a medium bowl, whisk together the flour, baking powder, and salt. Set aside.

3 In the bowl of a stand mixer fitted with a paddle attachment or a large bowl with a hand mixer, beat the almond paste and butter until creamy, about 1 minute. Add the sugar and beat for 2 to 3 minutes,

until light and fluffy. Add the eggs one at a time, mixing after each addition, then the lemon zest, and the almond extract. Mix for 1 to 2 minutes, until smooth and well incorporated. Turn the mixer to low, slowly add the flour mixture, and mix until just combined. The batter will be thick.

4 Scoop the batter into the springform pan and spread it evenly to the edges with a spatula. Scatter the sliced almonds in an even layer over the batter.

5 Bake for 40 to 45 minutes, until a toothpick inserted into the middle comes out clean. Remove from the oven and let cool on a wire rack for 20 minutes. Run a sharp knife around the edges before releasing the springform pan.

6 Before serving, sift powdered sugar over the cake. Garnish each slice with fresh berries and a dollop of whipped cream, if desired.

Make this!

To make 1 cup of cake flour, replace 2 tablespoons all-purpose flour with 2 tablespoons cornstarch, then whisk or sift to combine.

GOOEY BUTTER CAKE

I remember the first time I tried this dessert. It was April 14, 2011, at lunch on the set of *The Office*. There was a Gooey Butter Cake bake-off that day among the members of our St. Louis cast: Jenna Fischer, Phyllis Smith, and Ellie Kemper. I was one of the judges, and I unknowingly picked Jenna's as the best! As you can imagine, there was a big uproar because we are best friends. I honestly had no idea it was hers; it was just that good. Ever since that day, I have been a big Gooey Butter Cake fan. I mean, what's not to like? It's cake with a rich, buttery crust and a gooey, sugary filling. I'm in! As it turns out my husband makes a mean Gooey Butter Cake, too! So this recipe is in honor of my BFF and my favorite St. Louis gals: Jenna, Phyllis, and Ellie. —A

For the cake layer

1 (13.35-ounce) package yellow cake mix

¼ cup light brown sugar, packed

½ cup unsalted butter, melted and cooled to room temperature

2 large eggs, room temperature

½ teaspoon vanilla extract

½ teaspoon almond extract

For the cream cheese layer

8 ounces cream cheese, softened

½ cup unsalted butter, softened

2 large eggs, room temperature

1 teaspoon vanilla extract

4 cups powdered sugar, plus more for dusting

1 **Make the cake layer:** Preheat your oven to 325°F. Line a 13-by-9-inch baking dish with parchment paper. Set aside.

2 In a large mixing bowl, combine the cake mix, brown sugar, butter, eggs, vanilla extract, and almond extract. Mix until just combined, being careful not to overmix. Add the batter to the prepared baking dish and smooth it evenly across the top with a spatula.

3 **Make the cream cheese layer:** In another large bowl with a hand mixer or the bowl of a stand mixer fitted with the paddle attachment, beat the cream cheese and butter until creamy. Add the eggs and vanilla extract, mixing for 1 to 2 minutes, until everything is well incorporated. Gradually add the powdered sugar and mix thoroughly, scraping down the sides of the bowl as needed. Carefully scoop the cream cheese mixture over the cake batter, spreading it out to an even layer.

4 **Finish the cake:** Bake for 45 to 50 minutes, until the edges turn brown and crispy, while the center remains a bit soft and jiggly. Remove the cake from the oven and allow it to cool completely. For neatest slicing results, you might want to refrigerate it for an hour or two before cutting. Serve with a dusting of powdered sugar on top.

Make this!

Substitute the yellow cake mix with a chocolate or lemon cake mix for a different flavor profile.

CARROT CAKE *with* CREAM CHEESE FROSTING

This recipe is perfect for your spring gatherings. The natural moisture from the carrots gives the cake a wonderful texture and is incredibly flavorful. Our family is *big* on frosting, and this luscious cream cheese frosting transforms this dessert into something truly special!

For the cake

2¾ cups all-purpose flour

1 cup finely ground graham cracker crumbs, plus extra for decoration

1½ teaspoons baking soda

1½ teaspoons baking powder

1 teaspoon salt

1 tablespoon ground cinnamon

½ teaspoon ground nutmeg

½ teaspoon ground ginger

¼ teaspoon ground cloves

1½ cups canola oil

1½ cups granulated sugar

1 cup light brown sugar, packed

6 large eggs, room temperature

2 teaspoons vanilla extract

3½ cups grated carrots

½ cup canned crushed pineapple, drained

For the frosting

1 cup unsalted butter, softened

16 ounces cream cheese, softened

6 cups powdered sugar

2 teaspoons vanilla extract

1 to 2 tablespoons milk (2% or whole)

Candy carrots or icing carrots, for decoration (optional)

1 Make the cake: Preheat your oven to 350°F. Line three 8-inch round cake pans with parchment paper and lightly grease with nonstick or cooking spray. Set aside.

2 In a medium bowl, whisk together the flour, graham cracker crumbs, baking soda, baking powder, salt, cinnamon, nutmeg, ginger, and cloves. Set aside.

3 In a large bowl, whisk together the oil, granulated sugar, brown sugar, eggs, and vanilla extract until well blended. Slowly whisk in the flour mixture. Using a spatula, gently fold in the carrots and pineapple until nicely combined. Divide the batter equally among the three prepared cake pans.

4 Bake for 25 to 30 minutes, rotating the pans 180 degrees halfway through baking, until a toothpick inserted into the center comes out clean and the sides of the cakes pull away from the pan. Allow the cakes to cool in the pans. Once they are cool, gently remove them from the pans and place them on a flat surface. Level the tops using a cake leveler or a serrated knife to create even layers. Wrap the leveled cakes in plastic wrap and place them in the refrigerator or freezer for at least 30 minutes. Chilling the cakes makes them firmer and easier to frost.

SPRING
BREAK
trip to
HAWAII

5 **Make the frosting:** In the bowl of a stand mixer with a paddle attachment or in large bowl with a hand mixer, beat the butter until creamy. Add the cream cheese and continue beating until well combined and smooth, 1 to 2 minutes. Gradually add the powdered sugar, starting on low speed and increasing to medium speed, until light and fluffy. Add the vanilla extract, then the milk, a tablespoon at a time, and beat until very smooth and spreadable.

6 **Assemble the cake:** Place one of the cake layers cut side down on a cardboard round or serving plate. Scoop about ¾ cup of frosting onto its center and spread evenly to the edges. Place the second cake round on top and repeat this process. Add the final cake layer on top, again cut side down, and repeat, adding the frosting to the center and spreading it to the edges.

7 Once the three tiers are assembled, spread the frosting along the sides of the cake, smoothing the edges with a knife or an offset spatula, until the entire cake is covered with a nice thick layer of frosting.

8 With the palm of your hand, cup crushed graham crackers around the edge and over the top of the cake. Decorate the cake with candy carrots or icing carrots, if you'd like.

Chocolate PEPPERMINT CUPCAKES

A few years ago, Ange and I were guests on the *Rachael Ray Show* in New York City. We were asked to make one of our favorite recipes. It was around the holidays, so I knew these cupcakes would be perfect. We had a blast! Rachael and I even got into a powdered sugar fight. These cupcakes are rich and moist with a festive peppermint buttercream frosting, swirled with red gel and topped with a sprinkle of crushed peppermint candies. Rachael gave them two thumbs up. Not too shabby! (And for the record, she started the powdered sugar shenanigans.) —**J**

For the cupcakes

4 tablespoons unsalted butter

½ cup water

¼ cup canola oil

1 cup all-purpose flour

1 cup granulated sugar

⅓ cup unsweetened cocoa powder

½ teaspoon baking soda

½ teaspoon cornstarch

¼ teaspoon salt

1 large egg, room temperature

¼ cup buttermilk, room temperature

1 teaspoon vanilla extract

For the frosting

1 cup unsalted butter, softened

1 teaspoon vanilla extract

1½ teaspoons peppermint extract

½ teaspoon salt

4 cups powdered sugar

3 to 4 tablespoons heavy whipping cream

Red gel food coloring

¼ cup crushed candy cane

1 **Make the cupcakes:** Preheat your oven to 350°F. Line a 12-cup muffin tin with baking cups. Set aside.

2 In a microwave-safe bowl, microwave the butter, water, and oil together in 20-second intervals at half power, stirring after each interval, until the butter is melted. Let cool to room temperature.

3 In a large bowl, whisk together the flour, sugar, cocoa powder, baking soda, cornstarch, and salt. Add the melted butter mixture, egg, buttermilk, and vanilla extract and whisk until smooth. Using a ¼-cup measuring cup, pastry bag, or spoon, fill the baking cups to about three quarters full.

4 Bake for 20 to 22 minutes, until a toothpick inserted into the center comes out clean. Remove from the oven and allow to cool slightly in the tin before transferring to a rack to cool completely.

Christmas
BAKING *with*
RACHAEL RAY

5 **Make the frosting:** In a large bowl with a hand mixer or the bowl of a stand mixer with a paddle attachment, beat the butter until creamy. Add the vanilla extract, peppermint extract, and salt, mixing until well combined. Gradually add the powdered sugar, mixing on low speed. Add 2 tablespoons of the whipping cream, mixing until incorporated, then gradually add more cream until the frosting is smooth and fluffy, scraping down the sides of the bowl as needed. Increase speed to medium-high and beat for 1 to 2 minutes, until light and airy.

6 **Decorate the cupcakes:** Using a cupcake corer or sharp knife, hollow out the center of each cupcake to create a 1-inch pocket. Save the pieces you remove.

7 Fit a large piping bag with a large round tip. Swirl some red gel food coloring around the inside of the piping bag. Fill the bag with buttercream frosting. The red stripe inside will give the frosting a cool swirl effect. Pipe the frosting into the hole in each cupcake and top it off with the piece you cored out. Pipe more frosting on top in a decorative swirl pattern. Sprinkle the crushed candy cane on top to finish.

Make this!

To make 1 cup of buttermilk, combine 1 cup whole milk with 2 teaspoons lemon juice or vinegar and stir until combined.

Chocolate
Peppermint
Cupcakes,
page 220

Gingerbread CAKE POPS

Around three in the afternoon, I'm usually craving coffee. When the kids were little, their elementary school was near a Starbucks, so I'd pick them up and hit the drive-through line. One big coffee for me and three cake pops later, and everyone was feeling good about their day. Isabel, Jack, and Cade thought that only Starbucks made cake pops until I made my own one Christmas. Their minds were blown. This version blends the cozy, spiced flavors of gingerbread with a creamy white chocolate or colorful candy shell. They're perfect for parties, easy to transport, and sure to get everyone into the holiday spirit. —**J**

For the cake

1½ cups all-purpose flour

1 teaspoon baking soda

1 teaspoon ground cinnamon

½ teaspoon ground cloves

½ teaspoon ground nutmeg

½ teaspoon ground ginger

½ teaspoon salt

4 tablespoons unsalted butter, melted

¼ cup granulated sugar

¼ cup light brown sugar, packed

½ cup unsulfured molasses

¾ cup boiling water

1 large egg, room temperature

For the frosting

4 ounces cream cheese, softened

2 tablespoons unsalted butter, softened

1½ cups powdered sugar

1 to 2 teaspoons milk

1 teaspoon vanilla extract

For coating and assembly

12 ounces white candy melts

1 teaspoon coconut or canola oil

Holiday sprinkles

24 lollipop sticks

1 **Make the cake:** Preheat your oven to 350°F. Grease a 9-inch round cake pan with nonstick spray or cooking spray. Set aside.

2 In a medium bowl, whisk together the flour, baking soda, cinnamon, cloves, nutmeg, ginger, and salt. Set aside.

3 In a large bowl, whisk together the melted butter, granulated sugar, brown sugar, molasses, and boiling water until the sugar is dissolved. Allow to cool for a few minutes. Once it is cooled to room temperature, add the egg and whisk until well incorporated. Add the dry ingredients and stir with a wooden spoon or spatula until just combined. Pour the batter into the prepared pan.

4 Bake for 25 to 30 minutes, until a toothpick inserted into the center comes out clean. Remove from the oven and let the cake cool completely in the pan.

5 **Make the frosting:** In a large bowl with a hand mixer or the bowl of a stand mixer fitted with a paddle or whisk attachment, whip the cream cheese and butter until fluffy. Gradually add the powdered sugar, mixing on low speed until well incorporated. The mixture will be crumbly. Add the milk and vanilla extract, beating until smooth.

Recipe Continues

Gingerbread FUN *with* JOSH *and* CADE

6 **Make the cake pops:** Line a baking sheet with parchment paper. Set aside.

7 Once the cake is cool, with your hands, crumble it into fine crumbs into a large bowl. Add the frosting and continue to mix with your hands until it feels like wet sand. Using a cookie scoop or spoon, scoop about 2 tablespoons of cake mixture and roll with your hands to form a ball slightly bigger than a golf ball. Repeat with all of the cake mixture and place on the prepared baking sheet. You should have 24 cake balls. Chill in the refrigerator for 2 hours to set.

8 **Coat and assemble the cake pops:** When you're ready to prepare the coating, remove the cake balls from the refrigerator. In a microwave-safe mug or bowl, microwave the white candy melts as the package directs and thin with a bit of oil if needed. Make sure that whatever microwave-safe mug or bowl you melt them in has plenty of room to fully submerge each pop.

9 Dip ½ inch of the end of the lollipop stick or straw into the coating, then pause a moment to allow it to set. The tacky texture of the coating will act as a glue to keep the ball in place. Once the coating is still tacky to the touch but no longer runny, skewer a cake ball, stopping halfway through. Let sit for 1 to 2 minutes.

10 Dip each cake ball into the coating, tapping off any excess. You can also spoon on the coating to evenly cover the ball. Use the edge of the bowl or mug to smooth out the coating, then decorate with sprinkles. Stick the dipped cake pops into a Styrofoam block or cardboard box with holes punched in it to let the coating harden. Allow to set for 1 hour before serving.

Homemade FUNFETTI BIRTHDAY CAKE

There's something so nostalgic and whimsical about Funfetti. Simple yet festive, this homemade version of a childhood classic is perfect for birthdays or any other day that calls for a touch of fun.

For the cake

2¾ cups cake flour

2 teaspoons baking powder

½ teaspoon baking soda

1 teaspoon salt

½ cup unsalted butter, softened

½ cup canola oil

1¾ cups granulated sugar

1 cup buttermilk, room temperature

½ cup sour cream, room temperature

2 teaspoons vanilla extract

5 large egg whites, room temperature

½ cup rainbow sprinkles

For the buttercream

2 cups unsalted butter, softened

2 (2-pound) bags powdered sugar (about 8 cups)

2 teaspoons vanilla extract

½ teaspoon salt

2 to 4 tablespoons heavy cream or whole milk

¼ cup rainbow sprinkles, plus more for decorating

1 **Make the cake:** Preheat your oven to 350°F. Line two 8-inch round cake pans with parchment paper circles and grease with nonstick spray or cooking spray. Set aside.

2 In a medium bowl, whisk together the flour, baking powder, baking soda, and salt. Set aside.

3 In a large bowl with a hand mixer or the bowl of a stand mixer with a paddle attachment, beat together the butter, oil, and sugar until well combined. Turn the mixer to low, add half of the flour mixture, and mix until combined. Pour in the buttermilk, mix until combined, then add the remaining flour mixture and beat for 1 to 2 minutes until well incorporated. Mix in the sour cream and vanilla extract until just combined.

4 In a separate large bowl, whisk the egg whites vigorously until they form soft peaks. Gently fold the egg whites into the batter using a spatula. Fold in the rainbow sprinkles. Divide the batter evenly between the prepared cake pans and smooth the tops with a spatula.

ANGE'S backyard BIRTHDAY PARTY

5 Bake for 25 to 30 minutes, until a toothpick inserted into the center comes out clean. Once the cakes are cool, gently remove them from the pans and place them on a flat surface. Level the tops using a cake leveler or a serrated knife to create even layers. Wrap the leveled cakes in plastic wrap and place them in the refrigerator or freezer for at least 30 minutes. Chilling the cakes makes them firmer and easier to frost.

6 **Make the buttercream:** In a large bowl with a hand mixer or the bowl of a stand mixer with a paddle attachment, beat the butter on medium speed until creamy. Turn the mixer to low and gradually add the powdered sugar, 1 cup at a time. Increase speed to medium and beat until combined. The mixture might look a little dry. Add the vanilla extract, salt, and 2 tablespoons of heavy cream or milk, beating on medium high for an additional 1 to 2 minutes. Adjust with more cream or milk to reach a smooth, spreadable consistency. Fold in the rainbow sprinkles.

7 **Assemble the cake:** Place one cake layer cut side down on a serving plate or cake stand. Add a quarter of the frosting to the top and spread evenly to the edges. Gently place the second cake layer cut side down on top of the frosted bottom layer. Apply a thin layer of buttercream on top and around the sides of the cake. This layer, known as a crumb coat, helps seal in any crumbs and smooth out any irregularities, ensuring a cleaner final appearance. Chill the cake in the refrigerator for 15 to 30 minutes to set the crumb coat.

8 After the crumb coat has set, apply a generous layer of buttercream to the top and sides of the cake using an offset spatula or butter knife. Dip the spatula or knife into hot water and dry it off. Work quickly with the warm spatula to smooth the top and then the sides of the cake. Finish by sprinkling the cake with a cascade of rainbow sprinkles or even pressing the sprinkles around the sides of the cake. Chill until ready to serve.

Make this!

To make 1 cup of buttermilk, combine 1 cup whole milk with 2 teaspoons lemon juice or vinegar and stir until combined.

To make 1 cup of cake flour, replace 2 tablespoons all-purpose flour with 2 tablespoons cornstarch, then whisk or sift to combine.

Classic TEXAS SHEET CAKE

My Texas family is big on yearly family reunions. The locations are usually in the middle of nowhere, but my family doesn't mind. It's about "visiting," as my mom would say. Everyone brings a dish, and the meals are all potluck style and delicious. The one dessert I have vivid memories of is Texas sheet cake. Imagine a thin, brownielike cake topped with a rich chocolate ganache frosting (and if you ate my grandmother's, you got a serious sugar rush). It's perfect for kids' birthday parties or big family reunions. It feeds a crowd, and the sheet pan shape makes slicing and serving it a breeze. —**A**

For the cake

2 cups all-purpose flour

2 cups granulated sugar

1 teaspoon baking soda

½ teaspoon salt

1 cup unsalted butter

1 cup water

¼ cup unsweetened cocoa powder

½ cup buttermilk, room temperature

2 large eggs, room temperature

2 teaspoons vanilla extract

For the frosting

½ cup unsalted butter

¼ cup unsweetened cocoa powder

⅓ cup milk (2% or whole), room temperature

1 teaspoon vanilla extract

3½ cups powdered sugar

½ cup chopped pecans or walnuts (optional)

1 **Make the cake:** Preheat your oven to 350°F. Line an 18-by-13-inch rimmed baking sheet with parchment paper or grease with nonstick spray or cooking spray.

2 In a large bowl, whisk together the flour, sugar, baking soda, and salt. Set aside.

3 In a medium saucepan, melt the butter over medium heat, stirring. Once melted, whisk in the water and the cocoa powder. Whisk until the mixture is fully incorporated. Bring to a gentle boil, then immediately remove from the heat. Pour over the flour mixture and stir with a wooden spoon or spatula until just combined and smooth.

4 In a medium bowl, whisk together the buttermilk, eggs, and vanilla extract until the eggs are well beaten. Pour into the cocoa mixture and stir until just combined. Pour the batter onto the prepared baking sheet and smooth the top.

5 Bake for 20 to 22 minutes, until a toothpick inserted into the center comes out clean or with only a few moist crumbs attached.

ANGE *and*
her family
on the KINSEY
FARM

6 **Make the frosting:** Start the frosting when your cake has about 5 minutes left to bake.

7 In a medium saucepan, melt the butter over medium heat, stirring. Once melted, stir in the cocoa powder, milk, and vanilla extract. Whisk until combined and bring to a simmer. Remove from heat and gradually add the powdered sugar, whisking constantly until the frosting is smooth. If you're adding chopped pecans or walnuts, stir them in.

8 **Assemble the cake:** Remove the cake from the oven and pour the warm frosting over the top, spreading it out evenly with a spatula. Let the cake cool in the pan on a wire rack for at least 30 minutes before slicing. This helps the frosting set slightly and makes the cake easier to cut into neat squares. Serve directly from the pan. Enjoy!

Make this!

To make 1 cup of buttermilk, combine 1 cup whole milk with 2 teaspoons lemon juice or vinegar and stir until combined.

Gooey Chocolate
PUDDING CAKE

For our anniversary one year, the whole family went to the little Italian restaurant by our house, and lava cake was on the dessert menu. The kids were so tickled by the name and the fanciness of the experience that we ordered it for them. Well, they loved it and became obsessed with it. Josh created this version for us to make at home. We love loading ours with ice cream, chocolate syrup, and sprinkles. —**A**

For the cake

1 cup all-purpose flour

2 teaspoons unsweetened cocoa powder

½ teaspoon baking soda

½ teaspoon salt

¼ cup semisweet chocolate chips

4 tablespoons unsalted butter

¼ cup granulated sugar

1 large egg, room temperature

1 large egg yolk, room temperature

½ cup milk (2% or whole), room temperature

For the pudding

½ cup granulated sugar

2 teaspoons unsweetened cocoa powder

1 teaspoon cornstarch

⅛ cup unsalted butter, diced

⅓ cup boiling water

½ teaspoon vanilla extract

Powdered sugar, ice cream, chocolate sauce, and/or sliced strawberries, for serving (optional)

1 **Make the cake:** Preheat your oven to 350°F. Grease two 16-ounce ramekins with butter, nonstick spray, or cooking spray and place on a baking sheet lined with parchment paper.

2 In a medium bowl, whisk together the flour, cocoa, baking soda, and salt. Set aside.

3 In a microwave-safe bowl, microwave the chocolate chips together with the butter for 45 seconds at half power, then in 15-second increments at half power, stirring after each interval, until smooth. Allow to cool slightly, then transfer to a large bowl. Add the sugar and whisk until combined. Add the egg and egg yolk and whisk until smooth. Add the flour mixture, stirring until the batter is uniform, scraping down the sides of the bowl as needed. Add the milk and stir until just combined. Divide the batter evenly between the prepared ramekins.

4 **Make the pudding:** In a medium bowl, whisk together the sugar, cocoa powder, and cornstarch. Set aside.

5 To another medium bowl, add the butter and pour in the boiling water, stirring until the butter has melted. Add to the sugar–cocoa powder mixture and stir until the sugar dissolves. Stir in the vanilla extract. Divide the pudding mixture over the batter in the ramekins.

6 Bake for 18 to 20 minutes, until the top is set. Remove the cakes from the oven and let them rest for 10 minutes. While still warm, invert each ramekin onto a plate and wait another 5 minutes before removing the ramekin. Serve the cakes warm, topped with powdered sugar, ice cream, chocolate sauce, and strawberries, if desired.

LEMON-FILLED CUPCAKES
with Toasted Meringue

These light cupcakes are filled with delicious lemon curd. The citrus flavor is balanced with a fluffy, sweet meringue, toasted to a perfect golden brown.

For the cupcakes

1½ cups cake flour

½ teaspoon baking powder

¼ teaspoon baking soda

⅛ teaspoon salt

½ cup unsalted butter, softened

1 cup granulated sugar

2 large eggs, room temperature

1 tablespoon lemon zest

1 teaspoon lemon extract

½ teaspoon vanilla extract

½ cup milk (2% or whole), room temperature

¼ cup sour cream, room temperature

For the meringue

4 large egg whites, room temperature

1 cup granulated sugar

½ teaspoon cream of tartar

1 teaspoon vanilla extract

For assembly

Half of 1 (10.5-ounce) jar store-bought lemon curd (about ¾ cup)

1 **Make the cupcakes:** Preheat your oven to 350°F. Line a 12-cup muffin tin with baking cups.

2 In a medium bowl, whisk together the flour, baking powder, baking soda, and salt. Set aside.

3 In a large bowl with a hand mixer or the bowl of a stand mixer fitted with a paddle attachment, beat the butter until creamy. Add the sugar and mix on medium speed until light and fluffy, 2 to 3 minutes. Add the eggs one at a time, mixing after each addition, then the lemon zest, lemon extract, and vanilla extract. Beat until combined, scraping down the sides of the bowl as needed. Reduce speed to low and add half of the flour mixture and then the milk, mixing until combined. Add the remaining flour mixture, then the sour cream, and mix until just combined. Fill each muffin cup three quarters full. A ¼-cup measuring cup works well for this.

4 Bake for 18 to 20 minutes, until a toothpick inserted into the center comes out mostly clean. Remove from the oven and let cool completely.

5 **Make the meringue:** Fill a medium saucepan with a couple inches of water and bring to a boil over high heat. Reduce heat to medium low so the water is at a slow boil and place a medium glass bowl on top to create a double boiler. The bowl should not touch the water.

6 Add the egg whites, sugar, and cream of tartar to the bowl. Whisk constantly for about 5 minutes, until the mixture reaches 160°F on a candy thermometer. It will be glossy, slightly thickened, and smooth, with no sugar granules remaining. Remove from heat.

7 In the bowl of a stand mixer fitted with a whisk attachment or a large bowl with a hand mixer, beat the egg white mixture on low speed, gradually increasing to high speed, until stiff, glossy peaks form, 5 to 7 minutes. Reduce speed to low and add the vanilla extract. Mix until just combined.

8 **Assemble the cupcakes:** Transfer the meringue to a large piping bag with either a large star tip or a large round tip.

9 Using a cupcake corer or sharp knife, hollow out the center of each cupcake to create a 1-inch pocket. Save the pieces you remove.

10 Pipe or spoon about 1 tablespoon of lemon curd into each pocket, then trim the cut-out pieces as

needed and place back on the top to seal in the curd. Pipe a swirl of meringue onto each cupcake, then lightly toast it with a kitchen torch. Store in the refrigerator until ready to serve.

Make this!

To make 1 cup of cake flour, replace 2 tablespoons all-purpose flour with 2 tablespoons cornstarch, then whisk or sift to combine.

WHITE CAKE
with BUTTERCREAM FROSTING

This White Cake with Buttercream Frosting is where my cake-decorating days kicked off. The cake is light and fluffy, and the buttercream is smooth and easy to work with—perfect for piping or spreading. My hybrid frosting recipe mixes butter for flavor with a bit of shortening to keep it stable, so you get a creamy taste together with a consistency that holds up to decorating. It's a go-to cake that's great for any celebration, turning basic ingredients into something special every time. —**J**

For the cake

2¾ cups cake flour

2 teaspoons baking powder

½ teaspoon baking soda

1 teaspoon salt

1 cup buttermilk, room temperature

½ cup sour cream, room temperature

2 teaspoons vanilla extract

½ cup unsalted butter, softened

½ cup canola oil

1¾ cups granulated sugar

5 large egg whites, room temperature

For the frosting

1 cup unsalted butter, room temperature

½ cup vegetable shortening

6 cups powdered sugar, sifted

2 teaspoons vanilla extract

½ teaspoon salt

3 to 4 tablespoons heavy cream

Gel food coloring

1 **Make the cake:** Preheat the oven to 350°F. Line two 9-inch round cake pans with parchment paper circles and grease with nonstick spray or cooking spray. Set aside.

2 In a medium bowl, whisk together the flour, baking powder, baking soda, and salt until combined. Set aside.

3 In a small bowl, whisk together the buttermilk, sour cream, and vanilla extract. Set aside.

4 In a large bowl with a hand mixer or the bowl of a stand mixer with the paddle atttachment, cream the butter and oil together on medium speed for about 1 minute. Add the sugar and beat for 1 to 2 minutes. Spoon in half of the flour mixture and half of the buttermilk–sour cream mixture. Mix on low speed until combined, scraping down the sides of the bowl as needed. Add the remaining flour mixture and buttermilk–sour cream mixture and mix until just combined.

5 In a separate medium bowl, whisk or beat the egg whites until soft peaks form, about 3 minutes. Gently fold them into the batter. Divide the batter between the two prepared cake pans.

6 Bake for 30 to 35 minutes, until a toothpick inserted into the center comes out clean and the sides of the cake pull away from the edge of the pan. Remove the cakes from the oven and let them cool in the pan for 10 minutes before gently turning them onto a wire rack to cool completely. Once the cakes are completely cool, gently remove them from the pans and place them on a flat surface. Level the tops using a cake leveler or a serrated knife to create even layers. Wrap the leveled cakes in plastic wrap and place them in the refrigerator or freezer for at least 30 minutes. Chilling the cakes makes them firmer and easier to decorate

7 **Make the frosting:** Using a stand mixer with the paddle attachment or a large bowl with a hand mixer, beat the softened butter and shortening on medium-high speed for 1 to 2 minutes, until fluffy. Stop the mixer and add half of the powdered sugar, then turn the mixer to low speed (to avoid making a mess) and mix until the sugar is fully combined with the butter. Increase speed to medium and add the vanilla extract, salt, and 2 tablespoons of cream. Beat together for 2 to 3 minutes, until whipped, fluffy, and creamy. Stop the mixer and add the remaining powdered sugar. Mix on low speed to start and then increase to medium speed. Add the cream 1 tablespoon at a time until the frosting is a smooth, spreadable consistency.

8 **Assemble the cake:** Place one cake layer cut side down on a serving plate or cake stand. Add one quarter of the frosting to the top and spread it evenly to the edges. Gently place the second cake layer cut side down on top of the frosted bottom layer. Apply a thin layer of buttercream on top and around the sides of the cake. This layer, known as a crumb coat, helps seal in any crumbs and smooth out any irregularities, ensuring a cleaner final appearance. Chill the cake in the refrigerator for 15 to 30 minutes to set the crumb coat.

9 After the crumb coat has set, apply a generous layer of buttercream to the top and sides of the cake using an offset spatula or butter knife. Dip the spatula or knife into hot water and dry it off. Work quickly with the warm spatula to smooth the top and then the sides of the cake.

10 **Decorate the cake:** When you're ready to decorate the cake, divide the remaining buttercream into bowls. Add a few drops of gel food coloring at a time, mixing it thoroughly into the buttercream until you reach the desired color. Transfer to a piping bag fitted with a star tip. Use the remaining buttercream to decorate the cake, and have fun!

11 **Decorating tips:** Fill a piping bag fitted with a star tip with buttercream icing and practice piping on parchment paper to get a feel for the pressure needed. You can make intricate designs such as rosettes, shells, or borders, or draw pictures on the cake, which is what we like to do.

Make this!

To make 1 cup of buttermilk, combine 1 cup whole milk with 2 teaspoons lemon juice or vinegar and stir until combined.

To make 1 cup of cake flour, replace 2 tablespoons all-purpose flour with 2 tablespoons cornstarch, then whisk or sift to combine.

Pumpkin Spice CAKE

When is the right time to start baking pumpkin desserts? September? October? How about anytime you want? I can't get enough of pumpkin desserts, and this Pumpkin Spice Cake is no exception. Imagine carrot cake's autumn cousin—an incredibly moist, flavorful treat, topped with cream cheese frosting with a sprinkle of pumpkin spice for the perfect finishing touch. —**J**

For the cake

2¼ cups all-purpose flour

2 teaspoons pumpkin pie spice

1½ teaspoons ground cinnamon

1½ teaspoons baking powder

1 teaspoon baking soda

½ teaspoon salt

¾ cup canola oil

¾ cup light brown sugar, packed

¾ cup granulated sugar

1 (15-ounce) can pumpkin puree

4 large eggs, room temperature

2 teaspoons vanilla extract

¼ cup milk (2% or whole), room temperature

For the frosting

½ cup unsalted butter, softened

8 ounces cream cheese, softened

1 teaspoon vanilla extract

1 teaspoon pumpkin pie spice, plus more for dusting

3½ cups powdered sugar (about half of a 2-pound bag)

1 to 2 tablespoons milk (2% or whole)

1 **Make the cake:** Preheat your oven to 350°F. Line a 13-by-9-inch baking dish with parchment paper or grease with nonstick spray or cooking spray. Set aside.

2 In a medium bowl, whisk together the flour, pumpkin pie spice, cinnamon, baking powder, baking soda, and salt. Set aside.

3 In a large bowl with a hand mixer or the bowl of a stand mixer with the paddle attachment, blend the oil, brown sugar, granulated sugar, and pumpkin puree until well combined. Add the eggs and vanilla extract, mixing until well incorporated. Gradually add the dry ingredients, mixing just until combined. Don't overmix. Add the milk and mix until just combined with the batter. Transfer the batter to the prepared baking dish.

4 Bake for 35 to 40 minutes, until a toothpick inserted into the center comes out clean. Remove the cake from the oven and allow it to cool in the pan for 30 minutes. Once it is cool, cover loosely with plastic wrap and refrigerate for 1 to 2 hours before frosting.

5 **Make the frosting:** In a large bowl with a hand mixer or the bowl of a stand mixer fitted with a paddle attachment, beat the butter until smooth. Add the cream cheese and continue beating for about 30 seconds, until well combined. Mix in the vanilla extract and pumpkin pie spice, then gradually add the powdered sugar, starting on low speed and increasing to medium speed, beating until fluffy. Adjust the frosting consistency with milk, adding gradually until the frosting is smooth and spreadable.

6 **Assemble the cake:** Spread an even layer of the cream cheese frosting over the top of the cooled cake. Refrigerate the cake for an additional 30 minutes to set the frosting before slicing and serving. Garnish with a dash of pumpkin pie spice if desired.

STRAWBERRY POKE CAKE

While I was growing up in Kansas and Colorado, my mom and grandmother used to make this easy and delicious cake, and now I'm thrilled to share it with my kids. It is one of Isabel and Cade's favorite desserts! Parents, this is a great recipe to make with your kids. They will love poking the holes in the cake. —J

1 (14.25-ounce) box white cake mix, plus the ingredients called for on the box (e.g., neutral oil, eggs, water)

1 (3.3-ounce) box strawberry-flavored Jell-O mix

1 cup boiling water

1 cup cold water

8 ounces defrosted whipped topping (such as Cool Whip) or fresh whipped cream

Sliced strawberries, for garnish

1 Prepare and bake the cake in a 13-by-9-inch baking dish according to the package instructions. Let the cake cool for 15 minutes. Using a straw or the end of a wooden spoon, poke holes evenly across the entire cake 1½ inches apart.

2 In a medium bowl, combine the Jell-O mix and the boiling water. Stir until the mix has dissolved. Add the cold water and stir until combined. Pour evenly over the cake, making sure that it seeps into all the holes. Cover with plastic wrap and refrigerate for at least 3 hours, until the Jell-O firms.

3 Spread the whipped topping evenly over the top of the cooled cake and garnish with sliced strawberries. Keep refrigerated until ready to serve.

Whipped Cream

If you'd like to make your own whipped cream in place of using Cool Whip, you can use this recipe.

1 cup heavy cream

2 tablespoons powdered sugar

1 teaspoon vanilla extract

Chill a mixing bowl and beaters in the freezer for about 15 minutes. Pour the heavy cream into the chilled bowl and beat on medium-high speed. As the cream starts to thicken, add the powdered sugar and vanilla extract. Continue beating until stiff peaks form. Be careful not to overbeat, or the cream will become lumpy and butterlike.

Pies and Puddings

PIE CRUST

I'm not here to judge anyone's pie preferences—pie is pie, and it's all delicious! But I have to say, the pies that truly have my heart are the ones with a homemade flaky butter crust. Now, I know that making your own crust can seem a bit daunting and time consuming, and there's zero judgment if you use a store-bought one. But trust me on this: Our recipe takes just a little over an hour from start to pie-ready dough, and it makes a world of difference. Once you get the hang of making your own crust, you'll find it hard to go back to the store-bought variety. —**J**

2¾ cups all-purpose flour, plus more for dusting

2 tablespoons granulated sugar

1 teaspoon salt

1 cup cold unsalted butter, diced

Ice-cold water

1 In a food processor, pulse together the flour, sugar, and salt until combined. Add the butter and pulse until the mixture forms pea-size lumps. Drizzle in 2 tablespoons ice-cold water and pulse a few times. Check if the dough holds together when pinched. If it's crumbly, add more ice-cold water, a little at a time, pulsing after each addition, until the dough holds together.

2 Turn the dough out onto a lightly floured surface. Press the dough together and flatten into two equal-size 1-inch-thick disks. Wrap in plastic wrap and place in the refrigerator for about 1 hour.

❝ The pies that truly HAVE MY HEART *are the* **ones with a homemade FLAKY BUTTER CRUST.**

Chocolate MERINGUE PIE

I have only ever had one birthday dessert request, and that is for Chocolate Meringue Pie. My mom made it for me while I was growing up, and it is still my favorite. I don't even like sharing it; I eat the whole pie a slice a day (or eat it straight from the pie dish with a fork) to make it last as long as possible. I told this to Josh once when we were on a road trip. I remember it so clearly because it was the exact moment I found out that he also loves Chocolate Meringue Pie and his mom also made it for his birthday while he was growing up! That might have been the moment I knew I'd marry him. And are you ready for this? Josh got his mom's recipe (which is almost exactly like my mom's), and he makes it for me every year for my birthday. He doesn't even ask me to share it with him. Soul mate much? —**A**

For the crust

1 pie crust, store bought or homemade (page 244)

Egg wash (1 large egg mixed with 1 tablespoon water or milk)

For the filling

5 large egg yolks, room temperature

1¼ cups granulated sugar

⅓ cup cornstarch

⅓ cup unsweetened cocoa powder

½ teaspoon salt

2 cups whole milk, room temperature

2 tablespoons unsalted butter

2 teaspoons vanilla extract

For the meringue

5 large egg whites, room temperature

1⅓ cups granulated sugar

½ teaspoon cream of tartar

¼ teaspoon salt

½ teaspoon vanilla extract

1 **Make the crust:** Preheat your oven to 400°F.

2 If you are using a store-bought crust, follow the package instructions for a fully baked crust. If you are preparing a homemade crust, remove the dough from the refrigerator and place it on a lightly floured surface. Roll out the dough into a 12-inch circle ⅛ inch thick. Transfer the dough to a 9-inch pie plate, gently pressing it into the edges. Cut away excess crust, leaving about a 1-inch overhang over the edge of the pie plate all around. Fold the overhang under itself and flute or crimp the edges. Pierce the bottom of the dough with a fork a few times. Place a sheet of parchment paper into the pie crust and fill it with pie weights or dry beans.

3 Bake for about 12 minutes, until the edges are lightly golden. Remove from the oven and remove the parchment paper and pie weights. Brush with egg wash. Bake for another 10 to 12 minutes, until the crust is golden brown and fully baked. Let cool completely before adding the filling.

Recipe Continues

ANGE *with* her
birthday PIE

4 **Make the filling:** In a medium bowl, beat the egg yolks well with a whisk. Set aside.

5 In a medium saucepan, whisk together the sugar, cornstarch, cocoa powder, and salt. Over medium heat, whisk in the milk. Whisk constantly for 4 to 5 minutes, until the mixture comes to a simmer. Continue whisking about 1 minute, until the mixture thickens. Reduce heat to low. Slowly whisk a ladleful of the hot milk mixture into the egg yolks to **temper** them. Increase heat to medium and slowly whisk the tempered yolk mixture into the saucepan. Cook, stirring constantly, over medium heat for 1 minute, until the mixture is as thick as toothpaste. Remove from heat and whisk in the butter and vanilla extract until the butter is melted and the mixture is smooth. Pour into the baked pie crust and spread evenly. Cover with plastic wrap and press down gently to seal. Set aside to cool while you make the meringue.

6 **Make the meringue:** Fill a medium saucepan with about 2 inches of water and heat over medium heat until the water begins to simmer.

7 In the bowl of a stand mixer fitted with a whisk attachment, whisk together the egg whites, sugar, cream of tartar, and salt until thoroughly combined.

8 Place the bowl over the saucepan of simmering water to create a double boiler. The bottom of the mixer bowl should not touch the water. Whisk the mixture constantly until the sugar dissolves and the mixture thickens and becomes a little cloudy, with a light, foamy texture and the temperature reaches 160°F on a candy thermometer. This should take 3 to 5 minutes. Scrape down the sides of the bowl as needed to prevent burning. Remove from heat and stir in the vanilla extract. Return the bowl to the stand mixer and beat at medium-high speed for 5 to 7 minutes, until the mixture becomes cool and glossy and forms medium-stiff peaks.

9 **Assemble the pie:** Remove the plastic wrap from the pie. Using a spatula, spread the meringue evenly over the top of the chocolate mixture, sealing the edges of the crust completely so no moisture can seep in. Finish by making soft mountainlike peaks with the spatula.

10 Toast the meringue using a kitchen torch or pop the pie into the oven under the broiler for about a minute, just until it is a nice light golden color.

11 Let the pie cool on the counter for about 1 hour, then store in the refrigerator until ready to serve.

Classic APPLE PIE

Apple pie might seem like a common dessert, but the fun is in all the ways
you can make it your own. In our house, we love our apple pieces small and soft, almost
like a chutney or thick preserve made of a mixture of tart Granny Smith
apples and sweet, juicy Envy apples. I know some folks prefer big apple slices
with a bit of bite, and I get it; it's all about what you love. **—J**

For the filling

10 to 12 medium apples (a combination of Granny Smith, Envy, and Honey Crisp, or your favorite combinations), cored, peeled, and chopped into ½-inch pieces (about 8 cups)

½ cup lemon juice

⅓ cup unsalted butter

½ cup light brown sugar, packed

¼ cup granulated sugar

3 tablespoons cornstarch

2 teaspoons ground cinnamon

½ teaspoon ground nutmeg

½ teaspoon ground ginger

½ teaspoon salt

1½ cups water

1 teaspoon vanilla extract

For the crust

2 pie crusts, store bought or homemade (page 244)

Egg wash (1 large egg plus 1 tablespoon water or milk)

Coarse sugar, for sprinkling

1 **Make the filling:** In a large bowl, toss the apples and lemon juice together. Set aside.

2 In a large saucepan, melt the butter over medium heat. Stir in the brown sugar, granulated sugar, cornstarch, cinnamon, nutmeg, ginger, and salt. Add the water and bring to a low boil, stirring constantly. Cook for 2 to 3 minutes, stirring, until the mixture starts to thicken. Stir in the apples and simmer over medium-low heat for 10 minutes, stirring occasionally. Remove from heat, stir in the vanilla extract, and set aside to cool completely.

3 **Make the crust:** If you are using a store-bought crust, follow the package instructions for a fully baked crust. If you are preparing a homemade crust, remove the dough from the refrigerator and place it on a lightly floured surface. Roll out the first dough disk into a 12-inch circle ⅛ inch thick. Transfer the dough to a 9-inch pie plate, gently pressing it into the edges. Cut away excess crust, leaving about a ½-inch overhang over the edge of the pie plate all around. Roll out the remaining dough disk to the same dimensions as the first and cut it into strips about ½ to ¾ inch wide.

4 **Assemble the pie:** Pour the cooled apple filling into the pie dish over the bottom crust. Using the strips of dough, weave a lattice design over the apple filling and flute or crimp the edges. If you need some visual inspiration, there are many online videos that can show you how to create a lattice crust. Using a pastry brush, brush the top crust with egg wash and generously sprinkle coarse sugar over the top. Chill the pie in the refrigerator for 30 to 45 minutes before baking.

5 When you're ready to bake, preheat your oven to 400°F. Bake the pie on a baking sheet for about 20 minutes, until the crust starts to brown on the edges. Reduce heat to 350°F. Place a pie shield over the outside rim of the pie. You can make one out of aluminum foil or use a store-bought silicone version. Bake for 30 to 35 minutes, until the pie crust is golden brown. Let cool completely for at least 3 hours before cutting.

LEMON MERINGUE PIE

Ange calls me her "mountain man" because my heart will always belong to Colorado, but there is one thing I have grown to love about living in California: Lemon trees are everywhere. We have three in our yard, and I cook and bake with lemons from them all the time. In fact, when Ange asked me what I wanted for Father's Day last year, I asked, "Do we have room for another lemon tree?" If you are like my family and love a zesty lemon dessert, this pie is the ultimate treat! It's the perfect mix of sweet and tangy with a lusciously lemony filling inside a crust that's just the right blend of crisp and flaky. —J

For the crust

1 pie crust, store bought or homemade (page 244)

Egg wash (1 large egg plus 1 tablespoon water or milk)

For the filling

5 large egg yolks

1¼ cups water

1½ cups granulated sugar

⅓ cup cornstarch

½ cup fresh lemon juice

1 tablespoon lemon zest

½ teaspoon salt

3 tablespoons unsalted butter

For the meringue

5 large egg whites

1⅓ cups granulated sugar

½ teaspoon cream of tartar

¼ teaspoon salt

½ teaspoon vanilla extract

1 Make the crust: Preheat your oven to 400°F.

2 If you are using a store-bought crust, follow the package instructions for a fully baked crust. If you are preparing a homemade crust, remove the dough from the refrigerator and place it on a lightly floured surface. Roll out the dough into a 12-inch circle ⅛ inch thick. Transfer the dough to a 9-inch pie plate, gently pressing it into the edges. Trim the dough, leaving about a 1-inch overhang over the edge of the pie plate all around. Fold the overhang under itself and flute or crimp the edges. Pierce the bottom of the dough with a fork a few times. Place a sheet of parchment paper into the pie crust and fill it with pie weights or dry beans.

3 Bake for about 12 minutes, until the edges are lightly golden. Remove from the oven and remove the parchment and pie weights. Brush with egg wash. Bake for 10 to 12 minutes, until the bottom crust is golden brown and fully baked. Let cool completely before adding the filling.

4 Make the filling: In a medium bowl, whisk the egg yolks until frothy. Set aside.

Recipe Continues

Making *one* *of* MOM'S FAVORITES!

8 **Make the meringue:** Fill a medium saucepan with about 2 inches of water and heat over medium heat until simmering.

9 In the bowl of a stand mixer fitted with a whisk attachment, whisk the egg whites, sugar, cream of tartar, and salt until combined. Place the bowl over the saucepan of simmering water. The bottom of the bowl should not touch the water. Whisk constantly, until the sugar dissolves and the mixture thickens and becomes a little cloudy, with a light foamy texture. The temperature should reach 160°F on a candy thermometer. This should take 3 to 5 minutes. Make sure to scrape down the edges to prevent burning. Remove the bowl from the saucepan and stir in the vanilla extract. Return the mixture to the stand mixer. Beat at medium-high speed for 5 to 7 minutes, until the mixture becomes cool and glossy and forms medium-stiff peaks.

10 **Assemble the pie:** Remove the plastic wrap from the pie. Using a spatula, spread the meringue evenly on top of the lemon mixture, sealing the edges of the crust completely to avoid gaps where moisture can seep in. Toast the meringue using a kitchen torch or pop it in the oven under the broiler for about a minute, until it is a nice light golden color. Let the pie cool on the counter for about 1 hour. Then store in the refrigerator until ready to serve.

5 In a medium saucepan over medium heat, whisk together the water, sugar, cornstarch, lemon juice, lemon zest, and salt until blended. Continue whisking constantly for about 5 minutes, until the mixture bubbles and thickens. Make sure to scrape around the edges to prevent burning.

6 Remove from heat and temper the egg yolks by slowly adding a ladleful of the hot mixture into the egg yolks while whisking. Whisking vigorously, add the egg mixture to the saucepan and return the saucepan to the heat. Cook, stirring constantly, over medium heat for another minute until the mixture is thick and smooth.

7 Remove from heat and quickly stir in the butter until melted. Pour the lemon filling into the baked and cooled pie crust and spread evenly. Cover with plastic wrap, gently pressing it down on top of the lemon filling to seal. Set aside on the counter to cool while making the meringue.

Creamy CARAMEL CUSTARD (FLAN)

This custard is similar to flan and can be stored in the fridge for several days, making it a fantastic make-ahead dessert. So if you want to dazzle your friends at a dinner party, this is the dessert to try!

1 cup granulated sugar

⅓ cup water, plus 2 tablespoons

2 large eggs

4 large egg yolks

1 (14-ounce) can sweetened condensed milk

1 (12-ounce) can evaporated milk

½ cup half-and-half

1 tablespoon vanilla extract

½ teaspoon salt

1 Preheat your oven to 300°F. Prepare a roasting pan or 12-inch-square baking pan by lining it with a heat-safe cotton or linen kitchen towel and greasing four 10-ounce ramekins with butter. Set aside.

2 In a medium saucepan, combine the sugar and the ⅓ cup of water. Stir gently over medium heat until the sugar dissolves. Bring to a boil, then lower heat to medium low and simmer for 5 minutes without stirring (you don't want the sugar to crystallize). Increase heat to medium high and watch as the sugar turns golden brown, then remove from heat and gently swirl to even out the color. Carefully add the 2 tablespoons of water to stop the boiling, allowing the mixture to gently swirl together, and pour a quarter of the caramel into each prepared ramekin. Do not stir.

3 In a medium bowl, whisk together the eggs and egg yolks. Add the condensed milk, evaporated milk, half-and-half, vanilla extract, and salt and whisk until smooth. For an extra-smooth custard, strain this mixture through a fine-mesh sieve before you pour it into the ramekins.

4 Arrange the ramekins in the prepared roasting pan and create a water bath by pouring boiling water into the pan surrounding them, reaching halfway up their sides. Carefully place the roasting pan in the oven and bake for 1 hour 10 minutes to 1 hour 20 minutes. The custard should be set at the edges but still slightly wobbly in the center. Remove from the oven and let cool in the pan for 30 minutes. Once cool, remove the ramekins, dry them off, cover them with plastic wrap, and refrigerate for at least 4 hours (preferably overnight).

5 To serve, run a sharp knife around the edge of each ramekin, invert a plate over the top, and turn it over to release the custard. If the custards don't release on the first try, gently loosen the edges again with the knife. Drizzle any caramel retained in the ramekin on top.

Make this!

To ensure the even and gentle cooking process that is crucial for custard-based desserts, avoid opening the oven door frequently as fluctuations in temperature can cause cracks. After baking, a gradual cooling in the oven with the door ajar can prevent sudden temperature changes that might affect the texture.

Toasted PECAN PIE

In my family, no holiday is complete without pecan pie. This recipe, much like the one my grandmother used to make with pecans from her very own tree, is a sweet nod to my Texas family. My mom and sisters still make this recipe, and they are delighted that Josh is a big pecan fan. In fact, his love of pecans is so well known among my family that I can't tell you how many times he has unwrapped a birthday or Christmas gift to find a gallon-size zip-lock bag full of shelled pecans. So here is Josh's Toasted Pecan Pie to honor our families' love of pecans. Just the smell of it baking brings back sweet memories of my grandparents and the traditions we learned from them and continue to enjoy. —A

For the crust

1 pie crust, store bought or homemade (page 244)

For the filling

1½ cups raw pecan halves, divided

¾ cup golden syrup or dark corn syrup

½ cup light brown sugar, packed

½ cup granulated sugar

¼ cup pure maple syrup

3 tablespoons unsalted butter, melted and cooled to room temperature

1 teaspoon ground cinnamon

1 teaspoon vanilla extract

½ teaspoon salt

4 large eggs, room temperature

½ cup raw pecans, coarsely chopped

2 teaspoons granulated sugar

1 **Make the crust:** Preheat your oven to 400°F.

2 If you are using a store-bought crust, follow the package instructions for a parbaked pie crust. If you are preparing a homemade crust, remove the dough from the refrigerator and place it on a lightly floured surface. Roll out the dough into a 12-inch circle about ¼ inch thick. Transfer the dough to a 9-inch pie plate. Cut away excess crust, leaving about a 1-inch overhang over the edge of the pie plate all around and flute or crimp the edges. Pierce the bottom of the dough with a fork a few times. Place a sheet of parchment paper into the pie crust and fill the shell with pie weights or dry beans.

3 Bake for about 12 minutes, until the edges are lightly golden. Cool on a wire rack. Once cool, remove the parchment paper and pie weights. Decrease the oven temperature to 350°F.

4 **Make the filling:** Spread all of the pecan halves on a baking sheet in a single layer and toast in the oven for 6 to 8 minutes, until fragrant. Set aside to cool, reserving 1 cup for topping.

5 In a large bowl, whisk together the golden syrup or corn syrup, brown sugar, granulated sugar, maple syrup, butter, cinnamon, vanilla extract, and salt. Whisk in the eggs until the mixture is uniform. Add the chopped pecan pieces and ½ cup of pecan halves. Stir until they are evenly coated in the syrup.

6 **Assemble the pie:** Pour the filling into the baked pie shell and place on a baking sheet. Arrange the remaining pecan halves on top of the pie in a concentric circle pattern. Sprinkle the sugar over the pecans.

7 Bake for 40 to 50 minutes, until the edges of the filling have puffed and the center is still slightly jiggly. If the crust begins to brown too much, cover with foil or a pie shield and continue baking. Let the pie cool completely before slicing.

Classic PUMPKIN PIE

I'm obsessed with pumpkin everything, but nothing can compete with this Classic Pumpkin Pie. I don't need any fancy whipped cream toppings; just the basic combination of smooth, creamy pumpkin filling over a flaky, buttery crust, and I'm in Heaven. Here's my tip to avoid cracks on the top of your pie: Leave it in the oven with the door ajar and the heat off until it cools. —**J**

For the crust

1 pie crust, store bought or homemade (page 244)

For the filling

1 tablespoon all-purpose flour

1 tablespoon cornstarch

2 teaspoons pumpkin pie spice

½ teaspoon salt

1 (15-ounce) can pumpkin puree

1 (12-ounce) can evaporated milk

1 cup light brown sugar, packed

2 large eggs, room temperature

1 large egg yolk, room temperature

1 teaspoon vanilla extract

1 **Make the crust:** Preheat your oven to 400°F.

2 If you are using a store-bought pie crust, follow the package instructions for a parbaked crust. If you are using a homemade crust, remove the dough from the refrigerator and place it on a lightly floured surface. Roll out the dough into a 12-inch circle ⅛ inch thick. Transfer the dough to a 9-inch pie plate, gently pressing it into the edges. Cut away excess crust, leaving about a 1-inch overhang over the edge of the pie plate all around and flute or crimp the edges. Pierce the bottom of the dough with a fork a few times. Place a sheet of parchment paper into the pie crust and fill it with pie weights or dry beans.

3 Bake for about 12 minutes, until the edges are lightly golden. Cool on a wire rack. Once cool, remove the parchment paper and pie weights. Reduce the oven temperature to 375°F.

4 **Make the filling:** In a small bowl, whisk together the flour, cornstarch, pumpkin pie spice, and salt. Set aside.

5 In a large bowl, whisk together the pumpkin puree, evaporated milk, brown sugar, eggs, egg yolk, and vanilla extract until thoroughly combined. Add to the pumpkin mixture and whisk together until well mixed with no lumps.

6 **Assemble the pie:** Transfer the pumpkin mixture into the cooled pie crust, filling it about three quarters of the way. To prevent the edges of the pie from browning too quickly, place a pie shield over the outside rim.

7 Bake the pie for 50 to 55 minutes, until the pie is almost set in the center, with a very slight wobble. Turn off the oven and let the pie cool inside the oven with the door ajar until it reaches room temperature. Remove from the oven and continue to cool for about 3 hours at room temperature. This waiting is key to achieving the perfect texture.

Make this!

When using a 9-inch pie plate, this recipe will yield extra pumpkin filling; a 10-inch plate should fit just right. Use any leftover filling for mini pumpkin pies.

...2023

Hi Josh:

I thought you might like to have this picture I ran across when I was doing some cleaning.

It reminded me of how much you liked pumpkin pie—and you were in a hurry to get it.

It was taken at Great Grandma Pool's house

Hi to th...

Yes, it's
the cour...
just had
It is supp...
week how...

I do my wat...
stuff early in...
indoors durin...
I did a jigsaw...
aft...

Ye...
da...

supe...
you...
our t...
mor...

BABY JOSH *and a* sweet note
from GRANDMA SNYDER

Easy CHOCOLATE PUDDING

When my sisters and I were kids and we wanted a sweet dessert, my mom would whip up her famous chocolate pudding. It's a quick and easy treat you can enjoy hot or cold. The best part? You can customize it with coconut, extra chocolate, whipped cream, peanut butter, or caramel for that extra oomph. —**J**

½ cup granulated sugar

⅓ cup unsweetened cocoa powder

¼ cup cornstarch

½ teaspoon salt

2¾ cups milk (2% or whole), room temperature

2 tablespoons unsalted butter

1 teaspoon vanilla extract

Whipped cream and chocolate shavings, for serving (optional)

1 In a medium pot, whisk together the sugar, cocoa powder, cornstarch, and salt. Slowly whisk in the milk until smooth. Set heat to medium and continue whisking until the mixture begins to bubble and thicken. Reduce heat to low and cook, whisking, for 1 to 2 minutes, until thick. Remove from heat and add the butter and vanilla extract, stirring continuously, until the mixture is smooth and glossy. Transfer to a large bowl or individual ramekins. To prevent a skin from forming on top, place plastic wrap directly on the surface.

2 Chill in the refrigerator for about 2 hours. The flavors will develop and meld more fully as the pudding chills, so give it the full 2 hours or even a bit longer if you can wait. If you'd like, garnish with whipped cream and chocolate shavings before serving.

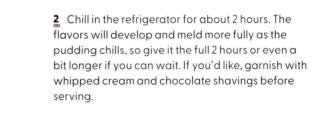

JOSH'S MOM
baking in the 80's

Easy KEY LIME PIE

Ange loves flowers, plants, and fruit trees. She is always bringing some plant home to add to our backyard, and one day she brought a tiny Key lime tree. She put it into a pot on the back porch, and we get beautiful little Key limes from it year-round. Isabel loves a citrus dessert, and this tangy recipe is one of her favorites. Prep tip: Roll the Key limes on the kitchen counter before squeezing to get the most juice out of them. —**J**

For the crust

1¾ cups crushed graham crackers

⅓ cup granulated sugar

½ cup butter, melted and cooled to room temperature

For the filling

2 (14-ounce) cans sweetened condensed milk

¾ cup Key lime juice (from about 20 Key limes)

½ cup sour cream, room temperature

1 tablespoon Key lime zest, plus more for topping

Fresh whipped cream, for topping

1 **Make the crust:** Preheat your oven to 350°F.

2 In a medium bowl, mix together the crushed graham crackers, sugar, and butter with a fork until the mixture reaches a uniform, sandy consistency. Press the mixture firmly into the bottom and up the sides of a 9-inch pie plate.

3 Bake for 10 minutes, until lightly browned. Cool completely on a wire rack.

4 **Make the filling:** In a separate medium bowl, whisk together the condensed milk, Key lime juice, sour cream, and Key lime zest until smooth.

5 **Assemble the pie:** Pour the filling into the cooled crust, smoothing the top with a spatula. Bake for about 10 minutes, until tiny pinhole bubbles burst on the surface of the pie. Cool completely on a wire rack, about 1 hour, then cover and chill in the refrigerator for at least 3 hours or, ideally, overnight.

6 Just before serving, top each slice with a big dollop of whipped cream and a sprinkle of Key lime zest.

Make this!

This recipe requires ¾ cup of Key lime juice, so you'll need between 20 to 25 Key limes. If you're using regular limes, which are larger, you might need 8 to 10. The final taste will be slightly different, but it will still be delicious.

Louisiana BREAD PUDDING *with* BOURBON SAUCE

Every time we make bread pudding, it feels like a sweet trip
back to my Louisiana roots. I was born in Lafayette, Louisiana, and still
have family there, and let me tell you, they know their way around a
kitchen! As my Aunt Brenda would say, "Sha, it's so good!" —**A**

For the pudding

1 loaf French bread,
cubed (about 6 cups)

3 large eggs, room
temperature

⅓ cup granulated sugar

½ cup milk (2% or whole),
room temperature

½ cup buttermilk, room
temperature

1 teaspoon vanilla extract

½ teaspoon ground
cinnamon

¼ teaspoon ground
nutmeg

For the sauce

½ cup butter

½ cup brown sugar,
packed

2 tablespoons bourbon

½ teaspoon vanilla
extract

⅓ cup chopped pecans,
for topping

1 **Make the pudding:** Preheat your oven to 350°F.
Lightly grease an 8-inch-square baking dish. Add the
cubed bread to the baking dish.

2 In a medium bowl, whisk together the eggs, sugar,
milk, buttermilk, vanilla extract, cinnamon, and
nutmeg. Pour the egg mixture over the bread and
toss until coated. Allow the mixture to rest for
5 minutes so the bread can absorb the liquid.

3 Cover the dish with aluminum foil. Bake for
30 minutes, remove the foil, and bake for 10 to 15
minutes, until the top is golden and crisp and the
custard is set. Allow to cool slightly while you prepare
the bourbon sauce.

4 **Make the sauce:** In a medium saucepan, stir the
butter and brown sugar over medium heat until the
butter has melted and the mixture is uniform. When
the mixture begins to bubble, remove from heat and
stir in the bourbon and vanilla extract. Pour the warm
sauce over the bread pudding and sprinkle with the
chopped pecans.

Make this!

To make 1 cup of buttermilk, combine 1 cup whole milk
with 2 teaspoons lemon juice or vinegar and stir until
combined.

Mason Jar BANANA CREAM PUDDING

Every time I eat this dessert, it takes me back to our wedding day. We wanted a simple wedding that felt like us, down home and casual with a rustic vibe. Josh found a beautiful venue in the Santa Monica Mountains. We got married on November 13 under a canopy of trees and twinkly lights, and our reception dinner was in a little cabin. Bluegrass music played while our family and friends ate off mismatched vintage plates and bowls. Our wedding planner, the amazing Beth Helmstetter, suggested charming mason jar desserts. We both love banana cream pudding, and it was the perfect dessert to go into a mason jar. The layers of creamy banana-vanilla pudding, whipped cream, and crunchy cookie bits looked so festive and tasted delicious! —A

For the whipped cream

2 cups heavy whipping cream

⅓ cup granulated sugar

1 teaspoon vanilla extract

For the pudding

1 (3.5-ounce) box instant vanilla pudding mix

1½ cups milk (2% or whole), room temperature

½ cup sour cream, room temperature

½ cup sweetened condensed milk

4 ounces cream cheese, softened

For assembling

1 (11-ounce) box vanilla wafer cookies, crushed

4 medium bananas, sliced into discs

1 **Whip the cream:** In a large bowl with a hand mixer or the bowl of a stand mixer fitted with a whisk attachment, whip the whipping cream on low speed until soft peaks form, about 3 minutes. Increase the mixer to medium and slowly add the sugar and vanilla extract. Beat until medium-soft peaks appear, about 1 minute. Remove 1 cup of the whipped cream and set aside. Cover the remaining whipped cream and refrigerate for 30 minutes.

2 **Make the pudding:** In a medium bowl, whisk together the pudding mix and milk until well blended. Set aside.

3 In a large bowl with a hand mixer or the bowl of a stand mixer fitted with a paddle attachment, beat the sour cream, condensed milk, and cream cheese for 1 to 2 minutes, until smooth and creamy. Add the pudding and beat until combined. Set aside.

4 Gently fold the reserved whipped cream into the pudding until no white streaks remain. Press a piece of plastic wrap on top of the pudding to prevent a skin from forming and place it in the refrigerator for 30 minutes.

5 **Assemble the pudding jars:** When you're ready to assemble the pudding jars, transfer the whipped cream and pudding to pastry bags.

6 In a half-pint mason jar, layer about 2 tablespoons of crushed vanilla cookies and 4 to 6 slices of banana. Pipe in a 1-inch layer of pudding followed by a 1-inch layer of whipped cream. Repeat the same four layers once again. The goal is to see neat stripes of each component. Finish by sprinkling crushed cookies on top of the last layer of whipped cream. Refrigerate at least 1 hour before serving. Top each with a whole vanilla wafer cookie and a banana slice, if desired.

Frozen Desserts and Sweet Snacks

No-Bake FROZEN LEMON CHEESECAKE BITES *with* RASPBERRY SWIRL

On the hottest days of summer, the last thing we want to do is crank up the oven. That's when no-bake recipes come to the rescue. These cheesecake bites are perfect for those sweltering days; just keep them in the freezer, and grab one whenever you need a treat.

For the crust

1¾ cups graham cracker crumbs (about 9 cracker sheets, crushed)

½ cup powdered sugar

½ teaspoon salt

½ cup unsalted butter, melted and cooled to room temperature

For the filling

16 ounces cream cheese, softened

¼ cup fresh lemon juice

1 tablespoon lemon zest

1 cup powdered sugar

½ teaspoon vanilla extract

½ cup raspberry preserves

1 Make the crust: Line an 8-inch-square baking dish with parchment paper, leaving a 1-inch overhang over two sides. Set aside.

2 In a medium bowl, stir together the graham cracker crumbs, powdered sugar, and salt until combined. Stir in the melted butter with a fork until the mixture reaches a wet sand–like consistency.

Transfer to the prepared baking dish, pressing it down firmly until it forms a solid, even layer. You can also use a small flat dish or baking pan to press it down.

3 **Make the filling:** In a large bowl with a hand mixer or the bowl of a stand mixer fitted with a paddle attachment, beat the cream cheese, lemon juice, and lemon zest until creamy. Add the powdered sugar and vanilla extract and continue mixing until smooth. Gently spread the cream cheese mixture over the graham cracker base in an even layer. Spoon a mound of raspberry preserves onto each of the four corners of the baking dish on top of the cheesecake layer. Using a toothpick or chopstick, swirl the preserves throughout the cheesecake, creating a marbled effect.

4 Freeze the dessert, uncovered, for at least 1 hour. Once frozen, use the parchment paper to lift the bites out of the pan. Cut them into squares and serve immediately.

CARAMEL CORN

During the holiday season, my mom always whipped up her famous caramel corn. As a kid, I was fascinated by the process, watching her stir the caramel and then quickly pour the boiling mixture over the popcorn. The timing was fun to watch! Now that I can make it myself, it's a bit of a sweet curse because I can't stop eating it. I recommend making a big batch for road trips. It's a great car snack! —J

16 cups popped popcorn (½ cup unpopped kernels)

1 teaspoon baking soda

½ teaspoon cream of tartar

1 cup butter

2 cups brown sugar, packed

½ cup corn syrup

2 teaspoons vanilla extract

Flaky sea salt, for topping

1 Preheat your oven to 225°F. Line two large baking sheets with parchment paper.

2 Place the popped popcorn in an extra-large bowl or large Dutch oven.

3 In a small bowl, combine the baking soda and cream of tartar. Set aside.

4 In a heavy-lidded saucepan, melt the butter over medium-low heat. Carefully stir in the brown sugar and corn syrup, being careful not to get sugar on the sides of the pot. Increase heat to medium and bring the mixture to a low boil without stirring. Reduce heat to medium low and cover the saucepan for 1 minute. Remove the lid and let simmer for 2 to 3 minutes or until the caramel reaches 250°F on a candy thermometer. Do not stir.

5 Take the pan off the heat and add the vanilla extract and the baking soda–cream of tartar mixture. It will bubble up vigorously. Continue stirring until the color changes from dark brown to light golden brown. Immediately pour over the popcorn. Stir until all pieces are evenly coated. You need to work fast! Transfer the popcorn to the prepared baking sheets, spreading it out in a single layer.

6 Bake for 50 to 60 minutes, gently stirring every 20 minutes. Remove from the oven and let cool for 30 minutes. Sprinkle with flaky sea salt and break up any large clumps before serving.

BUTTER TOFFEE PRETZELS

I have a soft spot for anything toffee or caramel, especially when it's mixed with something salty. So when Ange and I stumbled upon butter toffee pretzels at a candy shop, it was love at first bite. After a lot of trial and error, I finally nailed this homemade version. These pretzels hit the perfect balance of sweet and salty, lightly candied and dusted with almond flour for a hint of nuttiness. They're also fun to make, so get the kids into the kitchen for this one! Angela loves to give these as holiday gifts, too. Just put them into a mason jar, tie a bow around it, and you have a festive, delicious present for friends and family. —J

For the pretzels

4 cups minipretzels

¾ cup unsalted butter

1 cup granulated sugar

¼ cup light corn syrup

1 teaspoon salt

½ teaspoon baking soda

½ teaspoon cream of tartar

1 teaspoon vanilla extract

For the topping

2 tablespoons almond flour

2 tablespoons granulated sugar

1 teaspoon salt

1 **Prepare the pretzels:** Preheat your oven to 250°F. Line a large baking sheet with aluminum foil. Place an oven-safe wire rack over the sheet and spray with nonstick or cooking spray. Set aside.

2 To a large heat-safe bowl, add the pretzels. Set aside.

3 In a heavy saucepan, melt the butter over medium-low heat. Stir in the sugar, corn syrup, and salt, being careful not to get sugar onto the sides of the pot. Increase heat to medium and bring to a slow boil, stirring occasionally. Reduce heat to medium low and cover for 1 minute. Do not stir. Uncover and let boil for 3 to 4 minutes without stirring, until the mixture is a golden-brown color and reaches 300°F on a candy thermometer. Remove from heat and stir in the baking soda, cream of tartar, and vanilla extract. Expect a lot of bubbling.

4 Once the bubbling slows down, pour the hot toffee over the pretzels, stirring quickly and gently until each piece is well coated. Using tongs, carefully place the pretzels onto a cooling rack in a single layer. Make sure they're not touching one another.

5 Bake for 30 minutes. Cool for 30 minutes, then place in a large bowl.

6 **Make the topping:** In a small bowl, whisk together the almond flour, sugar, and salt. Sprinkle over the pretzels and mix gently until they are well coated. Enjoy!

7 The pretzels can be stored in an airtight container for up to three weeks.

CREAM CHEESE MINTS

While our parents were at work, my sisters and I spent our days with my Grandma Snyder at her house in Kansas. We would color, play games, tinker on the piano, and sing our hearts out. But the best activity by far was making Cream Cheese Mints. Grandma would set up stations around the dining table for each of us, complete with our own bowls of sugar and a selection of silicone molds to create whatever shapes we wanted. Not only did we get to be creative, but we also got to eat the scraps! Some mints were for her church functions or my grandpa's work events, but we always made some just for ourselves—usually a colorful mishmash that tasted amazing, even if they looked a bit wonky. **–J**

8 ounces cream cheese, softened

½ teaspoon peppermint extract

4 cups powdered sugar

Gel food coloring

Silicone mint molds (optional)

½ cup granulated sugar, plus extra for molds

1 In a large bowl with a hand mixer or the bowl of a stand mixer fitted with a paddle attachment, beat the cream cheese and peppermint extract until smooth and creamy. Gradually add the powdered sugar in batches, mixing after each addition, until smooth, scraping down the sides of the bowl as needed.

2 Once the sugar is fully incorporated, divide the mixture into three bowls. Add a few drops of food coloring to each. To avoid dying your hands, wear rubber gloves or mix using a spatula. Cover the colored dough tightly with plastic wrap and refrigerate for about 30 minutes, until firm.

3 Sprinkle the mint molds, if using, with granulated sugar.

4 Pour the sugar into a medium bowl. Scoop teaspoon-size balls and roll them through the sugar until well coated. Firmly press into the molds, then immediately release them and place the mints on wax or parchment paper to harden.

5 Keep the mint creations in a covered container in the refrigerator. Enjoy!

Make this!

If you don't have silicone mint molds, you can still make the mints by rolling teaspoon-size portions of dough between your palms until smooth, placing them on a wax paper-lined baking sheet, and gently pressing down on each one with a fork.

Easy FRIED ICE CREAM

When I was a kid, going out to eat at a restaurant was a big deal, and my all-time favorite place to go was Chi-Chi's. This popular midwestern chain served my absolute favorite childhood dessert: fried ice cream. Nowadays, there aren't many Chi-Chi's left in the United States, but I wanted to recreate this beloved dessert to share with my family. I took a few shortcuts, but my version brings back all the nostalgic flavors of my childhood. My kids are now obsessed with it, and trust me, your family will love this easy, fancy-looking treat, too! —**J**

3 cups (24 ounces) vanilla ice cream

2½ cups crushed cornflakes (about 4 cups uncrushed)

¼ cup light brown sugar, packed

2 teaspoons ground cinnamon

1 teaspoon salt

6 tablespoons unsalted butter

1 teaspoon vanilla extract

Whipped cream, chocolate sauce, sprinkles, and cherries, for serving

1 Line a baking sheet with parchment paper. Take the ice cream out of the freezer and allow it to soften for 5 minutes.

2 Using an ice cream scoop, quickly scoop 6 ice cream balls, each about ½ cup in size, and place on the prepared baking sheet. Place the baking sheet into the freezer and freeze until solid, 3 to 4 hours.

3 Using a food processor, pulse the cornflakes in short bursts until they are a coarse, sandlike consistency. You could also crush the cornflakes in a gallon-size zip-top bag using a rolling pin.

4 In a large bowl, stir together the cornflakes, brown sugar, cinnamon, and salt.

5 In a large skillet, melt the butter over medium heat. Add the cornflake mixture and vanilla extract to the skillet and sauté for 2 to 3 minutes, stirring constantly, until golden brown and crisp. Remove from heat, transfer to a large, shallow dish, and cool completely.

6 Once the ice cream is frozen solid and the cornflakes are cool, roll each ice cream ball through the cornflakes until fully coated. Place the coated ice cream balls back onto the baking sheet and return to the freezer for 30 minutes to firm up. Serve topped with whipped cream, chocolate sauce, sprinkles, and cherries.

WATERMELON SORBET

When the summer heat hits, this sorbet is our go-to frozen dessert. We like to use an ice cream maker to speed things up, but you can also just let the sorbet freeze in a freezer-safe pan. It's worth it.

1 cup granulated sugar

½ cup water

Juice of one lemon (about 3 tablespoons)

3 cups cubed seedless watermelon

1 Add the sugar and water to a small saucepan and bring to a simmer. Stir for about 1 minute, until the sugar dissolves. Remove the saucepan from the heat and stir in the lemon juice. Cool completely.

2 In a blender, blend the watermelon and cooled syrup until smooth. Pour into an ice cream maker and churn according to the manufacturer's instructions. Transfer to an airtight freezer container and freeze for at least 3 hours before enjoying.

ALWAYS READY *for* Summer

Sheet Pan OREO ICE CREAM CAKE

For Isabel's tenth birthday, she had her heart set on an ice cream cake from our favorite shop, and I said to myself, "How hard can it be to make ourselves?" It turns out, pretty hard. The layers took forever to freeze, the tall springform pan was finicky, and the cake started melting as I decorated it. This streamlined version is a game changer! No more struggling with a springform pan or worrying about the decorating. Plus, slicing it is a breeze. The sheet pan ensures even layers and quicker freezing times, making it far more practical and hassle free. So sit back and enjoy the party with this easy, crowd-pleasing dessert! —**J**

---

1 box chocolate cake mix, plus the ingredients called for on the box (e.g., neutral oil, eggs, water)

2 quarts vanilla ice cream

2 cups crushed Oreo cookies (about 20 whole), reserving a little for the topping

2 quarts chocolate ice cream

1 (12-ounce) jar hot fudge topping

1 (16-ounce) tub whipped topping, such as Cool Whip

---

1 Following the package instructions, prepare and bake the chocolate cake in an 18-by-13-inch rimmed baking sheet. Cool completely.

2 In a large bowl with a hand mixer or the bowl of a stand mixer fitted with the paddle attachment, whip the vanilla ice cream for about 1 minute, until it's spreadable but still frozen. Spread the ice cream over the cooled cake in an even layer. Scatter the crushed Oreo cookies over the ice cream. Cover with plastic wrap and place in the freezer for at least 2 hours, until solid.

3 In a large bowl with a hand mixer or the bowl of a stand mixer fitted with the paddle attachment, whip the chocolate ice cream for about 1 minute, until it's spreadable but still frozen. Carefully spread the chocolate ice cream over the Oreo cookie layer. Drizzle the hot fudge sauce over the chocolate layer. Cover and freeze for 1 hour.

4 For the final layer, evenly spread the whipped topping over the fudge. Sprinkle reserved Oreo crumbs evenly over the top. Cover the cake and freeze for 1 hour.

5 Before serving, set the cake out for about 10 minutes. Use a knife heated under hot water to slice the cake easily.

Acknowledgments

We want to acknowledge everyone who encouraged us along the way. Special shout out to our grandparents and parents who taught us how to cook and bake. To our families in Texas, Louisiana, Colorado, and Kansas—there are so many of you, and if we listed you all, we'd run out of space, but we love you! Thank you to our kids for trying out our new dishes and being super honest about whether they liked them or not. We're so grateful to our friends who told us to keep baking and to please bring them any extra desserts we made. Tam Vo, you have been helping keep Josh on track since high school. Your friendship and baking skills have been an amazing source of support for us and without you, we would have only about five posts on our Baking with Josh & Ange Instagram account. Tam, you are the best!

To our amazing team: Erin Malone, Adam Griffin, Noah Swimmer, thank you so much for making our dream of having our very own cookbook come true! Tess Finkle, you told us years ago we should make baking videos, and even helped us buy recording equipment. Thank you for always believing in us! To our fantastic food photography and recipe editing crew: Victoria Wall Harris, Brianna Beaudry, Cate Kalus, and Hannah Aufmuth, thank you for bringing our recipes to life on the page.

To our wonderful editor, Rebecca Strobel—thank you for guiding us through this process. Thank you for answering our gazillion questions, hopping on countless zooms to brainstorm with us, and for your thoughtfulness. We could not have done this without you!

To everyone at Gallery Books who made this book so much better: Jen Bergstrom, Aimee Bell, Sally Marvin, Mackenzie Hickey, Lauren Carr, Fallon McKnight.

And a BIG thank-you to all of you for watching our videos over the years, making our recipes, and buying our first ever cookbook! Your support keeps us going. The kitchen is the heart of our home, and we have loved sharing it with you.

—Ange & Josh

Index

About the Authors

ANGELA KINSEY is an actor best known for her work on all nine seasons of *The Office*, part of the cast who won two Screen Actors Guild Awards for Outstanding Performance by an Ensemble in a Comedy Series and a Daytime Emmy for the webisodes *The Office: The Accountants*. She has starred in several Netflix original movies and Hulu originals, and she is the coauthor of the number one *New York Times* bestseller *The Office BFFs*. She is a cohost of *Baking with Josh & Ange* with her husband, Joshua Snyder. Angela currently co-runs the Ramble media company, and cohosts the award-winning podcast, *Office Ladies* with her best friend, Jenna Fischer.

JOSHUA SNYDER is an actor, influencer, and self-taught baker with a passion for bringing people together through food. Originally from Colorado and Kansas, Josh grew up in a family of do-it-yourselfers. His acting career took off with roles in popular TV shows like *One Tree Hill*, *CSI: NY*, and *Without a Trace*, along with numerous national commercials.

In 2008, Josh became a father and, as a dad on a budget, he began teaching himself how to bake for his young sons—making cakes and cookies for birthdays and school events. What started as a necessity quickly became a passion, and by 2016, he and his wife, Angela, turned his love of baking into the YouTube show *Baking with Josh & Ange*. Their fun, approachable style and easy-to-follow recipes have built a thriving online community. Along the way, they've collaborated with brands like Whole Foods, Sunsweet, the Honey Board, and Purina.